# DATE DUE

Trésor

profondeur

Tresor de Priam découvert à 8½ mètres de profondeur

Taf. 193

Nº 3491  Nº 3492  Nº 3493  Nº 3494  Nº 3495  Nº 3495 a

Nº 3495 b  Nº 3495 c  Nº 3495 d  Nº 3495 e  Nº 3495 f  Nº 3495 g

$\frac{39}{100}$ grandeur naturelle

Nº 3601

Nº 3602

Nº 3603

Nº 3603 a

Nº 3603 b

⁵⁹⁄₁₀₀ ... aturelle

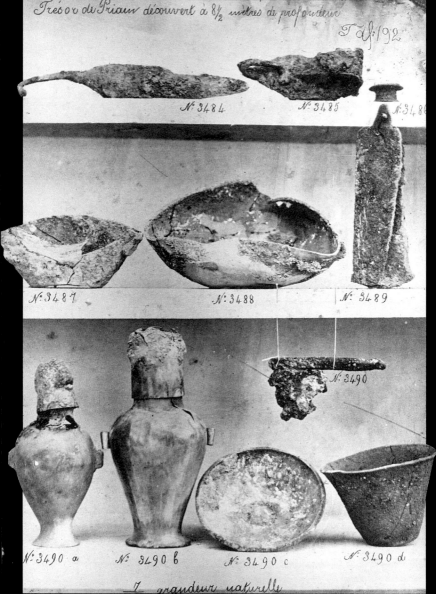

Trésor de Priam découvert à 8½ mètres de profondeur

Taf: 192

N: 3484

N: 3485

N: 3486

N: 3487

N: 3488

N: 3489

N: 3490

N: 3490 a

N: 3490 b

N: 3490 c

N: 3490 d

⅐ grandeur naturelle

Tafel 209

Trésor de

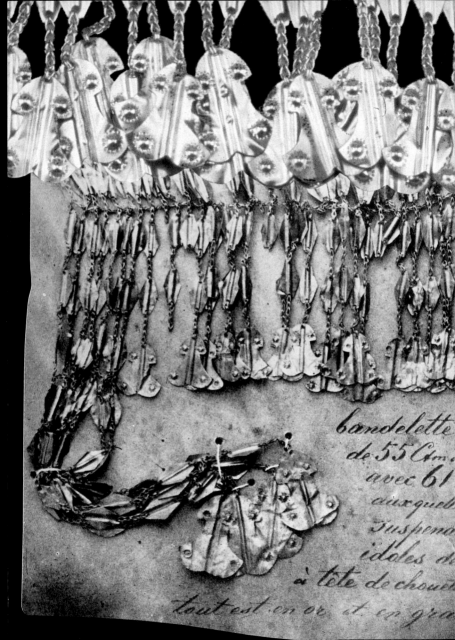

bandelette

de 55 C.m.

avec 61

auxquel

suspen

idoles d

à tête de chou

tout est en or et en gr

tête

...ng

...imes

...ont

... des

Minerve

la Θεὰ γλαυκῶπις Ἀθήνη d'Homère.

...leur naturelle

# CONTENTS

# THE GOLDEN
# TREASURES OF TROY
## THE DREAM
## OF HEINRICH SCHLIEMANN

Hervé Duchêne

THAMES AND HUDSON

"He combined business acumen and scientific zeal with the soul of a conquistador, whose personal El Dorado, stubbornly imagined, patiently unearthed, was the unexplored substratum of the Hellenic world. His poverty-stricken youth, his swift rise to fortune, his successful excavations—these are the stuff of fiction. If we did not possess the evidence of this triumph of one man's will, it would be difficult to believe."

Salomon Reinach
*Revue Archéologique*, 1891

## CHAPTER I
# A ROMANTICIZED BEGINNING

The ancient Greek poet Homer (opposite) was Heinrich Schliemann's sole guide on his voyage of exploration. It was Homer's *Iliad* and *Odyssey* that led the amateur archaeologist to the discovery of Troy.

Until quite recently biographers of Heinrich Schliemann (1822–90) faced a straightforward task. They had only to follow the man's own autobiography, scrupulously edited by himself and his wife, Sophia, or his commissioned biography. To illustrate his story they could draw on the personal reminiscences dotted throughout the writings (in many different languages) of the man who discovered Troy. They could mention Schliemann's taste for retsina (a Greek wine), his passion for bathing in the sea, and his habit of sending his shirts from Athens to London for laundering and ironing. They could recall Sophia Schliemann's stomach-aches and the moods of her Greek parents. As for the charges of improper practice, of manipulation, and of mythomania leveled at this controversial figure, they could safely be ignored. They were the

Braving academic scorn, the self-educated Schliemann had become a distinguished archaeologist. He had discovered Troy and Mycenae. His prestige in Europe, and particularly in Britain, was enormous. "I remain the hero of the hour," he wrote to his wife. "I am daily the guest of lords and dukes.… The painter [Sydney] Hodges is hounding me to pose for a life-size portrait [opposite]. He wants to exhibit it at the Royal Academy, and clearly thinks it will be a great feather in his cap to have painted Schliemann."

work of malicious minds, part of the eternal conspiracy of the intellectual establishment against the businessman.

By presenting his own story as a series of adventures, as the victorious struggle of an amateur archaeologist against the academic establishment, Schliemann fostered the birth of a myth: that of a pioneer spirit, a seeker of gold, a hero of fiction. A contemporary of the composer Richard Wagner, he staged his own life as if he were the leading actor in a second version of the *Ring*. Its prelude evokes a humble childhood peopled with legends inspired by German Romanticism and Greco-Roman myth. In three acts played out over the course of sixty-eight years, it portrays the businessman realizing his childhood dream of reawakening the Greece of the great poet Homer, and walking in the steps of the heroes of the epic poems the *Iliad* and *Odyssey*. The first act was apprenticeship. The second led to fortune. The third was inspired excavation.

The dream of uncovering the ruins of Troy was nurtured in the young Schliemann, so he later wrote, by an image of the city in flames (opposite), which he found in a children's history book. Homer's *Iliad* tells of the Greek siege of the fortified city on the coast of modern-day Turkey. According to Homer the Greeks finally succeeded in penetrating the walls through the "peace offering" of a wooden horse, which was, in fact, filled with Greek warriors.

Schliemann's point of departure was simple—a refusal to read the Homeric poems as mere stories. Flying in the face of accepted opinion, he perceived in them the building blocks of history. He gave them a geographical setting, that of the sites uncovered by excavation: Ithaca, Troy, Mycenae, Tiryns. He thus revived the Aegean world of the second millennium BC and became the father of pre-Hellenic archaeology. It was a field ablaze with objects such as the "Mask of Agamemnon" and the artifacts now collectively known as the "Treasure of Priam"—objects whose very names Schliemann fondly hoped would recall the heroic age

SAC DE TROYE

## Fame and Controversy

It is now a century since the death of this multilingual, self-taught man, who attained glory as an archaeologist despite the scientific community's hostility. The man and his discoveries still stand center stage. Today, in the age of Indiana Jones, Schliemann is the leading character of a novel, a play, and an opera. Irving Stone described his adventures in *The Greek Treasure*; Bruno Bayen's French play about the archaeologist, *Episodes Ignorés*, was staged in Paris in 1982; and the composer Betsy Jolas has just written an opera based on the play.

The man still stirs controversy. In 1972 the Stasi (the East German secret police) launched an inquiry into an unauthorized lecture delivered by a visiting American professor, William Calder III. Undaunted at the prospect of raising a storm, Calder had been rash enough to make some distinctly iconoclastic remarks as he stood by a Christmas tree in the vicarage where Schliemann was born a century and a half earlier. According to Calder the discoverer of the Homeric world had consistently blurred fact and fiction. The adventurer had lied to achieve his ends. A fog of doubt clouded his greatest successes. This

*Episodes Ignorés* (poster above), a play about Schliemann, ends with the disappearance of Berlin's Trojan collection in 1945. The "Treasure of Priam" eventually resurfaced in Moscow. The first meeting of Russian and German experts took place in 1994, under the aegis of the Pushkin Museum's director Irina Antonova (below).

two-sided view of Schliemann spurred renewed investigation of Berlin's most illustrious honorary citizen. And there remained one final indignity for Schliemann: the Berlin Wall had fallen, and the golden hoard of King Priam —donated by Schliemann in 1881 to the city of Berlin— now emerged from the cellars of Moscow's Pushkin

Schliemann's birthplace (left) in Neubuckow no longer exists. Heinrich did not live there long; in 1823 his father, Ernst Schliemann (below), became pastor of the village of Ankershagen. The black sheep of a long line of Lutheran ministers, Ernst (below) was a man of wavering loyalties and dissolute morals. Inheriting his father's energy, Heinrich felt a mixture of hatred, admiration, and exasperated affection for him. "Just the thought of being such a man's son," he later wrote, "fills me with fury."

Museum, after it had been assumed to have vanished without trace in the turmoil of the Second World War. Mystery thus continues to shroud Schliemann.

## A Grocer's Apprentice

Nothing in his early life suggested that Johann Ludwig Heinrich Julius Schliemann would one day become the founder of pre-Hellenic archaeology. He was born on 6 January 1822 in the little village of Neubuckow in Mecklenburg, northeastern Germany. He spent his first eight years in the even smaller hamlet of Ankershagen, between Waren and Penzlin, where his father, Ernst, was the Lutheran minister. Ernst quickly gained local notoriety by having an affair with one servant girl and marrying another soon after his wife's death from childbirth in March 1831. Learning of the scandal, his superiors forced him to abandon his ministry the following year. In his journal Heinrich describes his father as a mad dog, a tyrant as

cruel as Nero, a violent and hypocritical figure. Entrusted to the care of his uncle, a pastor at Kalkhorst, the boy entered the Neustrelitz vocational school in 1833. Yet after three years he broke off his studies, helping to support his debt-ridden family as apprentice to a grocer in Fürstenberg. When not sweeping the store he sold herring, butter, sugar, alcohol, and cooking oil.

According to Schliemann the only Greek he heard in those days were a few lines from the *Iliad* recited by a drunken miller: Homer in exchange for a stiff shot of whiskey! To hear the *Iliad,* Schliemann willingly dug into his pockets, pleased with this first business deal. In 1841 he was forced to leave his job at the store when he injured himself while shifting a heavy barrel. By now he dreamed of leaving for the New World, but his father refused to let him go. That summer Heinrich took a course in accounting at Rostock. Still finding himself drawn to the high seas, he signed on with a Hamburg merchant vessel bound for Colombia and Venezuela. The ship foundered off the Dutch coast, and Heinrich almost enlisted as a soldier in Amsterdam—before becoming an office boy in a trading house. But the young man quickly realized that the world is governed by those who can manipulate words and figures, and he was soon expert at juggling them. Exercising his memory as he ran his errands and spending his leisure hours learning languages, Schliemann mastered English,

Above: Faces of the Trojan War (Agamemnon, Achilles, Nestor, Odysseus, Diomedes, Paris, and Menelaus). According to Homer it was Paris, son of King Priam of Troy, who triggered the Trojan War by stealing the beautiful Helen, wife of the Greek King Menelaus. Below: The Trojan Aeneas fleeing his burning city with his father and his son.

French, Portuguese, and Italian in the space of a few months.

## Childhood Memories

But this picture does not always fit the mythic tone of Schliemann's own published childhood memories, which he slanted to support his later claim of a lifelong archaeological vocation. "The pickax and spade for the excavation of Troy and the royal tombs of Mycenae were already being forged and sharpened," he wrote. Heinrich regaled his six brothers and sisters and his friends Louise and Minna Meinke with tales of hidden treasure. Ankershagen was rich in such fables. A young woman bearing a silver chalice was said to emerge from the village pond at midnight. Not far from there, a robber baron had buried his son in a golden cradle; the whereabouts of his fortune remained a mystery. The family garden was haunted by the ghost of the previous tenant. A medieval castle nearby hid a thousand secrets in its cellars. Heinrich swore he would give Minna, his playmate and sweetheart, a share of his future spoils. True to his word, he remembered her in his will.

His father, who was neither a scientist nor an archaeologist but was passionately fond of ancient history, told his son of the tragic fate of Herculaneum and Pompeii, followed by their miraculous reappearance from beneath volcanic ash under the excavators' picks. The child also learned every exploit of Homer's warriors. One picture in particular spurred him to dream of rediscovering the remains of Troy. "My joy may be imagined, therefore, when I received from him [his father], in 1829, as a Christmas gift, Dr. Georg Ludwig Jerrer's *Universal History*, with an engraving representing Troy in flames, with its huge walls and the Scaean Gate, from which Aeneas is escaping, carrying his father Anchises on his back and holding his son Ascanius by the hand," he wrote in 1880. Despite his father's skepticism, Heinrich was convinced that the Trojan city would one day rise again. "If such walls once existed," he speculated,

"I think back with great fondness to our garden in Ankershagen, with its flowers, pears, cherries, plums, gooseberries, and the big lime tree where I carved my name. I remember too our church spire, from which I looked out over the world. I remember the verses my father wrote on the wall of our garden gazebo." How much truth is there in this recollection, penned by Schliemann in the course of an exercise in conversational Greek? In his autobiography Schliemann enticed his readers with childhood fables: "The gazebo was said to be haunted by the ghost of my father's predecessor, Pastor von Russdorf. Behind it was a pond." The family house (above) is today a museum to the hero.

"they cannot possibly have been completely destroyed: vast ruins of them must still remain, but they are hidden away beneath the dust of ages."

## Testing a Childhood Dream

The preface to Schliemann's *Ithaque, le Péloponnèse, Troie* (published in 1869) recalls another facet of this Trojan dream: "For Christmas 1832 I gave my father an account, in bad Latin, of the principal events of the Trojan War and the adventures of Odysseus and Agamemnon." His father's influence was decisive: "From the moment I could talk, my father told me the great exploits of Homer's heroes: I loved these stories; they held me spellbound; they fired me with enthusiasm."

Some today question this picture of childhood devotion and the ambition it is said to have kindled. As far as we know, Jerrer's *Universal History for Children* (with the famous engraving of Troy) is mentioned for the first time by Schliemann in a letter written in 1875, when he was fifty-three! And the presence in his library of an 1828 edition of Jerrer's book doesn't necessarily indicate the date of its acquisition. A handwriting expert asserts that the signature inside—"Heinrich Schliemann"—is not that of a child. The suggestion that this appealing tale was fabricated is strengthened by the fact that Schliemann actually borrowed the material for the Ankershagen legends—which had supposedly fueled his childhood daydreams—from a collection of tales first published in 1857. But the part played by the author's imagination in reconstructing his past counts for less than his concern to link this childhood to his passion for the Homeric world and his urge to disinter it.

Sigmund Freud pondered the Schliemann case. From his readings about Schliemann's excavations, he borrowed the image of successive levels of excavation to evoke the repository of our psychic impressions. In 1899 the psychoanalyst wrote to his friend Wilhelm Fleiss: "In discovering Priam's treasure this man found happiness, for only the fulfillment of a childhood desire can engender happiness." With the twin successes of the businessman and archaeologist in mind, Freud had noted in an earlier letter: "Happiness is the deferred realization

Sigmund Freud worked in Vienna surrounded by objects from antiquity (above). In 1899 he wrote: "I have bought Schliemann's *Ilios* and was fascinated by the story of his childhood."

Signs and symbols (opposite) intrigued Schliemann, who wrote an article in 1892 on the meaning of the swastika. In common use as far away as India, this emblem, suggestive of a wheel or of walking feet, seemed to him to be related to a primitive conception of solar movement.

of a prehistoric desire. That is why wealth plays so insignificant a part in it." That same year Freud congratulated himself on successfully concluding the analysis; he had reawakened a primordial episode buried in the unconscious of one of his patients. "It was as if Schliemann had once again uncovered the supposedly imaginary ruins of Troy," he wrote.

The archaeologist's life, therefore, can no longer be reduced to the handful of autobiographical facts he offers. The truth about the man and his achievement is emerging as unpublished archives surface, particularly those of the Gennadius Library in Athens. The mass of surviving documents is on a par with this outstanding personality: more than sixty thousand letters received or sent, hundreds of financial statements, and eighteen travel and archaeological notebooks—in all, thousands of pages written in ten different languages. A comparison of these sources with other recollections (his own and those of family and friends) is not to Schliemann's advantage. But the private person's subterfuges do not detract from the value of his discoveries. It matters little whether inventing a destiny for oneself implies weakness or genius. Heinrich Schliemann belongs to the race of great discoverers. We have only to follow his trail.

It took Schliemann just twenty years to achieve material success. The spoils of financial speculation would later help him to secure the treasures of knowledge—the gold of Troy. In the meantime, however, Schliemann donned an adventurer's guise. Leaving Amsterdam he established himself as a trader in Saint Petersburg, then traveled to California. His financial coups, like his stories, were partly the offspring of lies. Whether actually experienced or simply invented, his adventures would undergo a metamorphosis and become in his autobiographical self-portrait—the logical stages of apprenticeship.

## CHAPTER II
## INTERNATIONAL WHEELER-DEALER

Schliemann in 1860 (opposite); his German passport at the right. In the space of a year, Schliemann claimed to have more than doubled his investments. "Smug German grocer" was the French writer Maurice Barrès's acerbic comment.

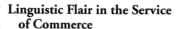

### Linguistic Flair in the Service of Commerce

On 1 March 1844 Schliemann was hired by the Amsterdam firm of B. H. Schröder & Company. As office boy he looked after the ledgers. His pay was initially skimpy, but he was hardworking and his zeal increased as his wages rose. He claimed to have begun the study of Russian with the help of a grammar book, a dictionary, and a translation of French writer François Fénelon's *Aventures de Télémaque*, an account of the voyage of Odysseus's son Telemachus. "So I betook myself to the study of it without a master, and, with the help of the grammar, I learned the Russian letters and their pronunciation in a few days. Then, following my old method, I began to write short stories of my own composition, and to learn them by heart. As I had no one to correct my work, it was, no doubt, extremely bad." Schliemann also paid a student (who spoke no Russian) to listen to him read. Six weeks after beginning his Russian studies, he was able to write a letter, in Russian, to Vassily Plotnikoff, the agent for Moscow's leading indigo traders. At public sales in Amsterdam, he negotiated discreetly with their emissaries.

Schröder (left), his Amsterdam employer, was the first to appreciate Schliemann's potential. Displaying the fullest confidence in him, the company dispatched him to Russia. Schliemann was grateful for this mark of esteem. Passport in hand, he left to explore Saint Petersburg and the Nevsky Prospekt (below). Schliemann began to teach himself Russian with a translation of François Fénelon's *Aventures de Télémaque* (map, below left).

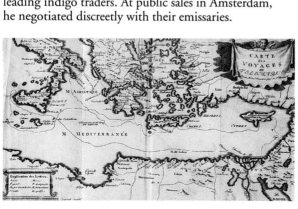

## Schliemann in Saint Petersburg

At the end of January 1846 Schröder & Company sent Schliemann to represent the firm in Saint Petersburg. The ambitious twenty-four-year-old successfully carried out his duties. On the side he did business on his own account, at first confining himself to indigo. "My business went so well," he wrote, "that in the beginning of 1847 I was inscribed in the Guild as a wholesale merchant." His only defeat was a sentimental one. Encouraged more by his improved social status than his bank account, he asked for the hand of his childhood sweetheart. It was too late; she was already married. "It had indeed happened to Minna and me as it often happens to us in our sleep, when we dream that we are pursuing someone and can never catch him, because as often as we reach him he escapes us again."

Despite his skills it took Schliemann several years to be

Schröder & Company's representative in Russia was at first a model employee, even taking care to husband his superiors' funds. He wrote to them: "I do not wish to occasion any expenditures until you have seen that the results of my efforts in the defense of your interests are truly worthy of compensation." But soon he was refusing to "work for one-half per cent in this magnificent Petersburg [below], the most expensive city in the world, where every step costs its weight in gold."

accepted into the closed circle of major Saint Petersburg merchants. But he had already opened a Moscow affiliate of his trading business. His reputation grew. "Here [in Saint Petersburg] and in Moscow I am considered the most clever, crafty, and competent merchant," he wrote to his father.

## Accidental American

In 1850 Schliemann left Russia for California. According to his autobiography, he spent two years there. "Not having heard of my brother, Ludwig Schliemann, who in the beginning of 1849 had emigrated to California, I went thither in the spring of 1850, and found that he was dead. Happening, therefore, to be in California when, on the 4th of July, 1850, it was made a state, and all those then in resident in the country became by that very fact naturalized Americans, I joyfully embraced the opportunity of becoming a citizen of the United States." In reality, however, Schliemann did not set sail for the New World until December 1850 and reached California only in the spring of 1851. As for American citizenship, he obtained it years later, in 1869. Similarly, despite the assertions in his travel diary, he probably never met the president of the United States or the "famous General Grant" or the governor of Panama. Some observers have seen in these fabrications just the start of Schliemann's later archaeological falsifications. Others have spoken of "psycho-pathic tendencies." Most certainly Schliemann lied and misled, but it is also possible that his intimate jottings —which initially were not intended for publication—

Schliemann's first wife, Katerina (above). This unflattering study probably mirrored the mood of a disillusioned husband, who wrote to her shortly after they were married: "How utterly reality, that grim specter, has destroyed my joyful hopes of yesteryear! You do not love me, and that is why you refuse to join in my happiness and remain indifferent both to my joys and my sorrows. You oppose me at every step, at every turn; worse, you accuse me of crimes that exist only in your imagination. Even thinking of it sets my hair on end and makes me shudder."

After the divorce Schliemann remained devoted to the children borne him by his Russian wife. His daughter Nadja (left) in 1863.

were no more than an exercise in style. His notebooks, a compendium of unusual or commonplace thoughts about the countries he visited, are a private world, the theater of his written apprenticeship in foreign languages. Schliemann, traveling always alone, dreamed of parallel lives, of escape from reality. Working by turns on his English and his Spanish, he told himself stories—both of his own adventures and ones he dreamed up.

His account of the fire that gutted San Francisco in the night of 4 June 1851 lends weight to this theory. At the time Schliemann was actually in Sacramento. Even if he had been in San Francisco, he could not have witnessed the disaster, which had, in fact, taken place one month earlier—in May. The date is of minor importance. More revealing are Schliemann's words, which are a first-person adaptation, down to the minutest detail, of an article in the 6 May *Sacramento Daily Union*. Improving his English by writing, Schliemann sought less to mystify unlikely future readers than to appropriate an event by telling it to himself.

The year 1854 opened brilliantly for Schliemann. "In expectation of future war," he wrote, "the prices of every kind of merchandise are soaring, and I made a large profit on a little coal deal concluded in a matter of half an hour." The Crimean War made his fortune. In 1855, a year after the Battle of Balaklava and the Charge of the Light Brigade, James Robertson took this photograph (below) of a port under blockade so favorable to the trader's interests—by Anglo-French and Turkish forces.

San Francisco ablaze (left). Schliemann claimed that he was asleep in the Union Hotel at the time. The noise outside awoke him and he saw the fire from the top of Telegraph Hill: "It was a frightful but sublime view, in fact the grandest spectacle I ever enjoyed." The truth is, he did not witness it. He simply dreamed up the account.

## Prospectors' Banker

In California Schliemann was unable to take over the land claim staked by his brother, who had died of fever at the age of twenty-seven. But his money bore fruit in Sacramento. He helped gold prospectors purchase supplies—by lending at a rate of twelve percent per month! His enterprise prospered. In September 1851 he joined forces with a San Francisco banker backed by the Rothschilds in London, and bought gold dust for cash at seventeen dollars an ounce. For eight months the precious metal—an average of eight thousand dollars worth each month—was ferried to San Francisco aboard the Gregory Express Company's steam trains, which returned to the gold fields with the cash.

Schliemann in his turn fell victim to fever, once in October and again in mid-January 1852. A third attack, at the end of March, prompted his departure. His partner accused him of cheating on the contents of the gold sacks and of setting up his own network on the side. On 7 April Schliemann sold his share to his associate. An announcement in the *Sacramento Daily Union* recorded the change of ownership. Schliemann left California much richer than when he had arrived.

*Your Obedient Servants,*

# H. SCHLIEMANN & Co.,

Bankers, in the Brick Building Cor. J and Front Streets.

## Dead Languages and Travel

In May 1852 Schliemann left New York and eventually returned to Saint Petersburg. On 12 October 1852, in the Orthodox Cathedral of Saint Isaac, he married Katerina Petrovna Lyshin, the daughter of a Saint Petersburg lawyer. It was an unhappy marriage, which produced three children: Sergei, born in 1855, Natalie, born in 1859 (she died at the age of ten), and Nadja, born in 1861.

The Crimean War of 1854–6, pitting Russia against Turkey (in alliance with Britain and France), made Schliemann's fortune. He delivered supplies, military equipment, and strategic materials (saltpeter, sulfur, lead) to the czar's armies. Only business, he told friends, made his life bearable. But business also brought its share of

L etterhead (opposite below) and advertisements in the *Sacramento Daily Union* are reminders of the days when Schliemann, from his brick office building, functioned as banker to adventurers and gold panners (below). As he told friends, "I always get up at 5 o'clock in the morning, take at 5 1/2 my breakfast in the Orleans Hotel and open my office at 6 o'clock to shut it at 10 o'clock in the

anguish—as on the day in 1854 when our hero believed he had lost everything. The Anglo-French blockade of Russia's ports made it necessary to land all goods in Prussia and then ferry them overland to their destination. On 4 October the neutral city of Memel in Lithuania (site of Schliemann's warehouses) was gutted by fire. Fortunately the flames spared his goods and, by an apparent miracle, his investment remained intact. Ironically, his profits were swollen by the fact that "capitalists were afraid to do much business during the Crimean War." By the end of the fighting, his earnings had more than doubled in a year.

evening.... My bank is from early till late constantly jammed, crammed, and rammed full of people from all nations and I have to speak all the day long in eight languages."

With Russia once more at peace, and with his fortune made, he began to learn modern Greek in 1856, using a translation of Bernardin de Saint-Pierre's romantic novel *Paul et Virginie*. He apparently feared at first that "this language would exercise too great a fascination over me and estrange me from my commercial business." But within several months he had mastered ancient Greek as well, and both the *Iliad* and the *Odyssey* were familiar reading. He took lessons from a Greek theological student, Theokletos Vimpos. The two men became friends, and fate was later to intertwine their lives. In the summer of 1858 Schliemann resumed his study of Latin, broken off when he left school in Ankershagen, and soon mastered its difficulties. This passion for the ancient world was not a pretense. "I believe a man can live without business activities," Schliemann wrote his father, "and before settling down I would like to visit the countries of southern Europe, particularly my beloved Homer's homeland, where I'll speak the new Greek language the way I speak German." This is the first indisputable reference to an interest in Homeric poetry and the land that gave it life.

Left unscathed by the economic crisis of 1857, Schliemann was tempted to liquidate his business assets. Deciding, in the end, against this step he began to travel, going first to Sweden and Denmark. Next he traveled through the East, keeping up a travel diary in six languages. For the return trip from Constantinople to Saint Petersburg, he took the Danube route. His crossing of the Dardanelles provided him with a first glimpse of the Troad—the area surrounding the ancient city of Troy. But the plain that had witnessed the battles of the *Iliad* excited the traveler less than his journey up the Nile, or the desert between Cairo and Jerusalem, or his visit to Petra (in modern Jordan). Admittedly, Schliemann had to cut short his trip. As he wrote, "After Syria I visited… Athens, in the summer of 1859, and I was on the point of starting for the island of Ithaca when I was seized with fever…. I therefore hurried to Saint Petersburg."

Above all, however, he needed to defend himself against charges of fraud brought against him by Stefan Soloviev, one of his debtors who had declared bankruptcy.

The businessman in Saint Petersburg (opposite) in 1860 and a bill of the same year recording the import of an American cotton consignment. Schliemann was eager to learn modern Greek and, as was his habit, he refused to study grammar, apart from declensions and verbs, relying chiefly for his progress on the recitation of selected passages. He was proud of his fluent written and spoken command of the language of Homer: "I am perfectly acquainted with all the grammatical rules without even knowing whether or not they are contained in the grammars; and whenever a man finds errors in my Greek, I can immediately prove that I am right, by merely reciting passages from the classics where the sentences employed by me occur." Once settled in Greece Schliemann cultivated a conversational Greek in the Homeric manner —which could surprise his contemporaries. Philologists (language experts) who have studied his doctoral dissertation at the University of Rostock agree on the quality of his Latin as opposed to the peculiarities of his Greek.

*238   1860.*

*Note of Cotton imported by Mr Henry Schliemann of St Petersburg*

*pr "John Ra...l"*

*Cotton   288.056   Tons 12.5*

*84*

Apparently in good health once more, Schliemann set off again in August, bound for Spain. But the outcome of Soloviev's suit remained uncertain for a long time and Schliemann had to resume his business activities. The secret of his success was importing on a large scale—and his unwillingness to trust middlemen. "I never confided the sale of indigo to clerks or servants, as others did, but always stood myself in my warehouse, and showed and sold it personally and wholesale to the indigo dealers." The indigo merchant had by now diversified into other fields: oil, tea, and cotton—once again a profitable business, as a result of the blockade of southern ports during the American Civil War in 1861.

Two years later Schliemann won his lawsuit on appeal. In December he began dissolving his Saint Petersburg business: "I found myself in possession of a fortune such as my ambition had never ventured to aspire to." His archaeological destiny beckoned.

"At last I was in a position to fulfill the dream of a whole lifetime—to visit at my leisure the theater of the events that had so powerfully interested me. I accordingly left in April 1868 …and visited one by one the sites where the poetic memories of Antiquity are still so fresh."

Heinrich Schliemann
*Ithaque, le Péloponnèse, Troie*, Preface, 1869

# CHAPTER III
# IN SEARCH OF A DESTINY

A 19th-century engraving (opposite) showing Muslim graves on top of the so-called Tomb of Achilles. For Schliemann, *Odyssey* in hand, this was indeed the Greek hero's resting place. A scene in Yokohama (right) from the time of Schliemann's visit.

## A Barbarian in Asia

"I have an immense urge to see the world," Schliemann wrote in a letter of May 1864. His Asian voyage, beginning that December and lasting six months, took him from India to China and Japan, and ended in San Francisco. This journey—decisive for his intellectual development—represented a double break: from the Russian business world and from his wife, with whom his relationship had long since deteriorated. The journey also charted his future course. In 1867 he began his first

The Great Wall of China (below) impressed Schliemann. "It silently protests," he wrote, "against the corruption and decadence that has fallen on the Chinese Empire."

book, *La Chine et le Japon au Temps Présent* (*China and Japan Today*). Written for a Saint Petersburg paper, it was based on the wanderer's travel journal; Schliemann also kept up a voluminous correspondence during the voyage. Private jottings, letters, and press accounts were all grist for his embryonic work. His later archaeological writings would evolve in the same fashion.

Enthusiasm rarely deserted Schliemann and he willingly set himself an exhausting schedule. In one day, in a series of forced marches, he reached and marveled at the Great Wall of China. He was as thrilled by the spectacle of nature as he was moved by the beauty of monuments and the diversity of foreign customs. His romantic soul delighted in descriptions of trees, flowers, and birds. He was awed by the Himalayas: "The prospects were too vast, too sublime. I simply stood there, overwhelmed by the beauty of the landscape."

Businessman Schliemann continued to watch his

LA CHINE
ET
LE JAPON
AU TEMPS PRÉSENT
PAR
HENRY SCHLIEMANN

PARIS
LIBRAIRIE GÉNÉRALE

1867

*China and Japan Today*, brought out in French by a small Paris publisher, was the fruit of Schliemann's travel diary (above). The explorer was spellbound by Chinese theater (below).

expenses. He bought only second-class tickets on the Indian railways. He complained if the food was bad and haggled over hotel rates. Nor did he forget his own financial interests. He used letters of recommendation and of credit to purchase consignments of indigo and tea; he visited a silkworm farm. At Yokohama in Japan he railed against the exchange rates: "The Japanese government has in its wisdom devised this refined form of corruption in order to impose the most crying injustices on foreign trade."

His travels also brought the pleasures of writing: "One is always so happy, contented, and focused while writing," he observed. "And in company one always has a thousand and one interesting things to impart, which invariably—as the fruit of long research and long reflection—amuse everyone."

## Sorbonne Student

Schliemann reached France in the first days of 1866, at the conclusion of an around-the-world trip. "I have…settled down in Paris," he wrote, "to study archaeology, henceforth with no other interruption than short trips to America." But this decision did not deter him from going to Moscow in March and traveling through Bavaria and Switzerland until mid-October. Initially he nurtured some hopes of attempting a reconciliation with his wife, then resigned himself to their separation. He speculated in real estate in a Paris whose layout had been newly configured by Baron Georges-Eugène Haussmann in the fading years of the Second Empire. By the start of the academic

In Paris Schliemann moved into a private townhouse at 6 Place Saint-Michel. He attended the Sorbonne (facade, below), and made friends with the great historian Joseph-Ernest Renan (below left).

year Schliemann, by now a wealthy property owner, was a student at the Sorbonne, taking courses in Asian languages, embarking on Egyptology, and studying Sanskrit. He had a first taste of Greek and Arab philosophy, of classical poetry, of contemporary French literature, and of comparative grammar.

He then broke off his studies and departed on a business trip to the United States, where he invested in railroads and bought land in Cuba. In a diary packed with figures

and business addresses, Schliemann praised the American spirit of enterprise, although he worried that freeing the slaves would reduce their productivity by a third. He recorded various visits: to schools, factories (particularly meat-packing plants), and cemeteries. He was haunted by the face of death, but even more so by the memory of his vanished brother, whose grave he never found.

At the end of January 1868 Schliemann returned to his studies at the Sorbonne, as well as to lectures at the Collège de France and meetings of scientific societies. In April he considered resuming his business activities in

Émile Burnouf (below) played a major part in Schliemann's intellectual development. An academic specializing in comparative mythology and author of the first French-Sanskrit dictionary, Burnouf was also a renowned Hellenist. From 1867 to 1875 he directed the French School at Athens. At one point Schliemann thought of leaving his Trojan gold to France; Burnouf served as intermediary, meeting with the French authorities, but an agreement was never reached. Burnouf's friendship with Schliemann began with the fifty letters that Burnouf sent him, along with flattering articles, and active help in the Trojan digs. It was Burnouf's task to record the depths at which each object was unearthed.

Russia in order to be near his children. In a letter to his son he outlined a journey intended to take him to Saint Petersburg via Switzerland, Italy, Greece, Turkey, Odessa, Kiev, and Moscow. But on learning that his Saint Petersburg associates had again initiated legal proceedings against him, he decided to delay his return to Russia. Nevertheless he set off—but southward. The ruins of ancient Rome and Pompeii had roused his curiosity.

## Tourism and Archaeology

It all began with a pleasure jaunt. On 5 May Schliemann turned up at Rome's Piazza del Popolo as an "ordinary tourist," aware that he lacked the knowledge necessary to carry out scientific activities. The traveler's journal conveys the swift awakening of his passion for archaeology. During his four weeks in Rome Schliemann divided his time equally between the monuments of antiquity and more modern sights. He approached the former through the intermediary of historical figures who intrigued him, such as Cleopatra or Nero. His fascination with the tyrant impelled him to explore the Domus Aurea, Nero's palace. He admired the Temple of Castor and Pollux. Yet there was a distinct touch of naïveté to his enthusiasm. He even believed, for example, that he had seen the fig tree where Romulus and Remus, the legendary founders of Rome, were abandoned!

Twenty days in the Bay of Naples introduced the apprentice archaeologist to the realities of antiquity. He visited Baia, Stabies, Cumae, and Capua, and above all Pompeii. He made two expeditions to the last site, attended a series of lectures, and marveled at the paintings uncovered during excavation and put on display at the Naples Museum. He was impressed by a meeting with Giuseppe Fiorelli, who was directing the dig and concentrating—and this was an innovation—on

stratification, the principle of classifying excavated material by layers. On 1 July Schliemann was at Messina in Sicily. Although always aware of Homer's writings —he confided to his diary that Lake Avernus is mentioned in the *Odyssey* and recorded the opinions of a guide who placed the Cyclops' cave in Sicily—the traveler gave more space in his notes to a mishap on Etna. Not far from the volcano's summit, his guide slipped away during the night. Schliemann had to climb on alone. He reached his hotel, under his own steam, the next day!

His journey to the Greek mainland began with a stop at Corfu on 6 July. After visiting Ithaca Schliemann met a fellow German in Athens on 25 July, the architect Ernst Ziller, who had been working

In Rome, by the columns of the Temple of Castor and Pollux (opposite above), Schliemann recalled the abyss that opened under the Forum and into which Marcus Curtius leapt in self-sacrifice to his death.

The grace and spontaneity of Pompeian frescoes (left: Achilles at Skyros) charmed Schliemann. He also admired the excavations (above) undertaken by Giuseppe Fiorelli. He marveled at Fiorelli's ability to bring the doomed Pompeians back to life by injecting plaster into the impressions left by their bodies.

Schliemann spent several days in Constantinople (modern Istanbul, left), awaiting the return steamer after his second visit to the Troad.

Diploma from the University of Rostock (opposite above), conferring a doctorate on the author of *Ithaca, the Peloponnese, Troy*. Seven hundred copies of the book were printed.

in the Troad. The meeting with Ziller was decisive. When he learned of the excavations under way and of the various theories about the site of ancient Troy, Schliemann set sail for the Dardanelles. While waiting for his ship, he busied himself visiting the plain of Argos—including Tiryns and Mycenae—where he hoped one day to uncover the tomb of King Agamemnon.

### Ithaca, the Peloponnese, Troy

In Paris that September Schliemann wrote *Ithaque, le Péloponnèse, Troie* (*Ithaca, the Peloponnese, Troy*), which was published in French at the author's expense at the beginning of 1869. It was the central component of an archaeological dissertation that earned him a doctorate from the University of Rostock in Germany.

The book was a blend of literary references and travel notes. Its tone was often lyrical. It shows us the traveler sleeping on Ithaca, a bank of stones for a bed and

VIRUM PRAENOBILISSIMUM

# HENRICUM SCHLIEMANN

TRADITO LIBRO ARCHAEOLOGICO
DE ITHACA INSULA PELOPONNESO ET TROADE

## PHILOSOPHIAE DOCTOREM ARTIUMQUE LIBERALIUM MAGISTRUM

ORNATUM ESSE

### PUBLICO HOC DIPLOMATE

CONFIRMAT

Homer's poems for a pillow. It tells us that the islanders warmly thanked their visitor for a public reading. There, "every hill, every rock, every fountain, and every olive grove breathe Homer and his *Odyssey,* and we are carried at one leap into the most resplendent era of Greek chivalry and poetry." He had borrowed this gust of enthusiasm from an English tourist guidebook; likewise the breathless (but fictitious) account of an attack by dogs in the south of Ithaca.

The fact remains that Schliemann carried out his first digs on the island of Ithaca and tested his methods there. Attempting to find Odysseus's palace on Mount Aëtos, he sought to locate the events of the Homeric epic in the landscape around him, to match the written record to the topography. The results were disappointing, but the novice was not discouraged. He now dreamed of identifying the sites described in the *Iliad* and *Odyssey,* confident that he had recognized "the mistakes of nearly all the archaeological explorers concerning the site once occupied by the Homeric capital of Ithaca, Eumaeus's stables [where Odysseus once stayed], the isle of Asteris, ancient Troy, the tombs of Batieia and Esyetes, Hector's tomb, etc." Unearthing a handful of urns, Schliemann

"We climbed Mount Aëtos [on Ithaca] on its western slope, which was a little less steep than the two other approaches. Many traces of an old pathway were visible, apparently leading from Odysseus's palace to the little port now known as Saint Spiridion." Schliemann was mistaken in thinking he had rediscovered the palace of Homer's hero on the mountain. He had explored the site of ancient Alalcomenae, an archaic-era settlement, traces of whose Cyclopean walls have survived (engraving of Ithaca, below).

naively exclaimed: "It is quite possible that these five little urns of mine contain the bodies of Odysseus and [his wife] Penelope or their descendants!"

Despite its defects, *Ithaca, the Peloponnese, Troy* attracted the interest of a university review board. The theory Schliemann proposed was indeed innovative. In a return to the traditions of antiquity—and in the face of contemporary opinion—he intended to seek Homeric Troy on the hill of Hissarlik in the territory of the Ottoman Empire (modern Turkey). Since Jean-Baptiste Lechevalier's initial exploration of the Troad, carried out in 1795, researchers had confined their activities to a nearby site at the Turkish village of Bunarbashi. Schliemann proved that this was a dead end. Whatever the experts believed, the writers of antiquity had not placed the Greco-Roman city of Ilium—the heir of Homer's Troy—at Bunarbashi, whose topography did not match the descriptions in the *Iliad.* Digging there had brought no conclusive results.

However, Schliemann only became slowly convinced of the possibility of Trojan ruins on the Hissarlik site. His travel diary shows that he himself also situated them initially at Bunarbashi. He began to suspect their presence on Hissarlik only after an encounter with the American Frank Calvert, who was preparing to leave the Troad. Calvert, the son of the United States vice-consul in the Dardanelles, was an amateur archaeologist and owned some of the land at Hissarlik. He had made promising preliminary probes there. *Ithaca, the Peloponnese, Troy* paid homage to this shrewd pathfinder. But while endorsing Calvert's opinion, Schliemann reserved the lion's role in the book for himself— presenting himself as standing alone against the scientific community, with a combination of lucidity, boldness, and intuition. However, it would be more accurate to suggest that Schliemann, having welcomed the ideas of other men, then managed to forge his own brand of certainty by giving himself time to think in Paris. His conviction was rational. He came to it while writing his book, after extensive reading, and correspondence with his American counterpart. The Hissarlik hypothesis was to prove a shrewd assessment.

Unsung hero of the Hissarlik digs: the American Frank Calvert (above). He was the first to realize that the hill was "largely artificial, and had been formed by the ruins and debris of temples and palaces built one on top of the other over long centuries."

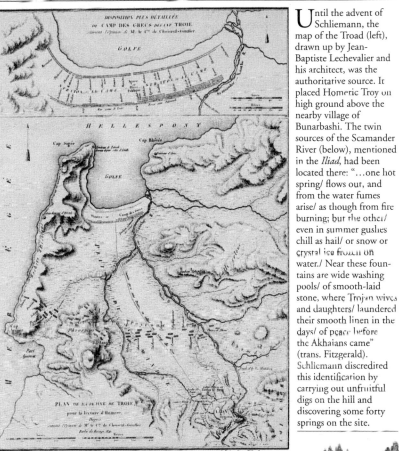

U ntil the advent of Schliemann, the map of the Troad (left), drawn up by Jean-Baptiste Lechevalier and his architect, was the authoritative source. It placed Homeric Troy on high ground above the nearby village of Bunarbashi. The twin sources of the Scamander River (below), mentioned in the *Iliad*, had been located there: "...one hot spring/ flows out, and from the water fumes arise/ as though from fire burning; but the other/ even in summer gushes chill as hail/ or snow or crystal ice frozen on water./ Near these fountains are wide washing pools/ of smooth-laid stone, where Trojan wives and daughters/ laundered their smooth linen in the days/ of peace before the Akhaians came" (trans. Fitzgerald). Schliemann discredited this identification by carrying out unfruitful digs on the hill and discovering some forty springs on the site.

"If my memoirs now and then contain contradictions, I hope that these may be pardoned when it is considered that I have revealed a new world of archaeology. The objects which I brought to light by thousands are of a kind hitherto never or but rarely found. It was an entirely new world for me; I had to learn everything by myself and only by and by could I attain the right insight."

Heinrich Schliemann
*Troy and Its Remains*, Preface, 1875

## CHAPTER IV
# HOMER'S LAND, PROMISED LAND

Sophia Schliemann (Heinrich's wife, opposite), adorned with jewels from the "Treasure of Priam." The urn (right), which Schliemann believed was decorated with an owl's head, graced the title page of his *Trojanische Alterhümer* (*Atlas of Trojan Antiquities*).

The conversion of the new initiate to archaeology was accompanied by a change in civic status: In 1869 Schliemann became an American citizen. In the same year he divorced his Russian wife and married again, in Athens. With the support of his friend Frank Calvert he began to explore Hissarlik in April 1870. For the next twenty years, in the course of seven intermittently conducted digs, he laid bare the remains of Troy and with it the "Treasure of Priam," revealing superimposed layers of ruins dating from successive eras of habitation. He extracted thousands of objects, swiftly trumpeting his discoveries and demonstrated a truly scientific interest in earthenware and in stratification. The man was a pioneer.

At a time when Delos, Olympia, and Delphi still awaited the

archaeologist's pickax, he began a series of "campaigns" that would bring Greek civilization back to life. Thanks to his bold research the Greek past, which until then could be traced back no further than the traditional date of the first Olympic Games in 776 BC, was now firmly located in the second millennium BC.

In 1874 Schliemann began excavating in the northeast Peloponnese; two years later he uncovered the gold of the Mycenaean tombs and the "Mask of Agamemnon." His dream was approaching fruition. Schliemann believed he had demonstrated that the Homeric texts did indeed reflect historical reality, and he used those texts to interpret the unknown Greece he was bringing to light. He thus claimed to have established a clear relationship between the architectural remains of the second millennium BC and the world described in the *Iliad* and the *Odyssey*. The approach had its weaknesses, for it blurred the line between real experience and events described in Homer's epics. But with Schliemann archaeology became a science; digging was now elevated to the status of an experiment designed to validate a theory.

Schliemann (opposite) —a United States citizen. Below: The Trojan plain and 1873 excavations. "If I may say so, the hill is now more impressive-looking than ever," wrote Schliemann. "The trenches and banks of rubble give it the look of some great fortress. The onlooker standing on the walls of the site sees below him a kind of immense caldron, at whose bottom sits the burned city with her walls and her house foundations as distinct as if marked out on a chart. From such a vantage point he can gain precise knowledge of the peculiar nature of the structures."

Reaching New York on 27 March 1869, Schliemann began the process of naturalization (below). United States citizenship came with startling swiftness: His new papers reached him two days later. On 1 April he was in Indianapolis, where the obstacles to divorce were easily surmountable. Four days later he applied for his divorce and a hearing was set for 30 June. He bought a house (left) for $1,125 and invested a further $12,000 in a factory. These investments were meant to show the judge that he had settled in the country. Yet in April he had already made plans to marry in Greece, launching an investigation into the character of his intended and bombarding Sophia's uncle with questions.

## Sentimental Education

Schliemann spent much of the year 1869 in the United States. As an American citizen he traveled to Indianapolis to take advantage of local legislation facilitating divorce. His own divorce became final in June, and three months later he married Sophia Kastromenos, daughter of a Greek cloth merchant. He had selected the seventeen-year-old girl from a photo album put together by his Saint Petersburg friend who had taught him Greek, Theokletos Vimpos, an Orthodox priest and uncle of the bride. Schliemann wrote to him: "I believe that a woman whose character

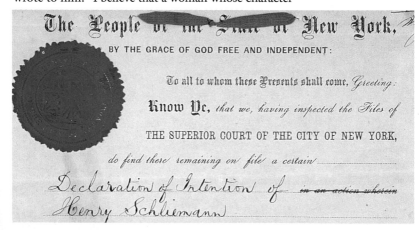

The People of the State of New York,

BY THE GRACE OF GOD FREE AND INDEPENDENT:

To all to whom these Presents shall come, *Greeting:*

Know Ye, *that we, having inspected the Files of*

THE SUPERIOR COURT OF THE CITY OF NEW YORK,

*do find there remaining on file a certain*

*Declaration of Intention of* ~~in an action wherein~~ *Henry Schliemann*

agreed wholly with mine, and imbued with my own love for the sciences, could respect me. And since she would remain my disciple her whole life long, I dare to hope that she would love me firstly because love is born of respect, and secondly because I shall endeavor to be a good teacher and shall devote all my free time to helping her in her quest for philological and archaeological knowledge."
Like Pygmalion, Schliemann dreamed of shaping his creation in order to unite knowledge and beauty. But things were not to be so simple. After a honeymoon in Paris, the Schliemanns returned to Athens in early February 1870. There a disappointment awaited them. Official Turkish permission to dig at Hissarlik—which they had requested before leaving for Paris—had not materialized. Heinrich left for the Greek Cycladic Islands, alone. This excursion put the finishing touches on his archaeological training and rounded out his knowledge of the major sites. He

Above: The Acropolis of Athens at the time that Heinrich and Sophia (below) were wed.

The Cyclades (the island of Syros, left, at the turn of the century) were Schliemann's destination when he left Athens on 27 February 1870. He stopped in Delos, soon to be explored by the French School at Athens. Directed by Emile Burnouf, the School was in the Lemnian House (below), on the site of the present Hotel Grande Bretagne. Schliemann reached Santorini only shortly before the French archaeologists. In April 1870 the latter were to find traces of houses dating from the second millennium BC. This unsuspected prehistoric past and the super-imposition of geological strata on the site excited Schliemann's curiosity. Like the tourists in the area (who were already numerous), he must have admired the pumice beds and the eastern port of Nea Kameni (opposite above, 1866 engraving).

visited Syros, Delos (where excavations did not begin until 1873), Paros, Naxos, and Santorini. Renewed volcanic activity on Santorini in 1866 had spurred increased scientific research there. Uniting the skills of volcanologists and archaeologists, work proceeded under the aegis of the French School at Athens. The material uncovered by excavation embarrassed the experts, for it bore no resemblance to anything so far encountered. Geological evidence appeared to place it in the first half of the second millennium BC, which seemed implausible. No comparative yardstick yet existed—but Schliemann's Trojan and Mycenaean digs would soon provide one.

Still waiting for news of his authorization to dig in the Troad, Schliemann postponed plans for another month. He organized family outings to Attica and the Peloponnese. Then, unable to wait any longer, he set off for the Dardanelles on 10 April. Although still without permission to excavate, he began a preliminary probe on the northwest corner of

Hissarlik to determine the depth of the topsoil. Sinking a sixteen-foot shaft, he uncovered a series of Roman and Hellenistic walls. Digging was halted at the end of the month when the owners of the site objected.

Sophia took no part in this work. She was absent the following year as well, giving birth in Athens to a baby girl, Andromache. Yet Schliemann wrote in his diary: "My dear wife, an Athenian lady who is an enthusiastic admirer of Homer, and knows almost the whole of the *Iliad* by heart, is present at the excavations from morning to night." However, she was indeed present during the 1872 season, throughout the month of June. Life on the work site was not without danger. Schliemann mentions the accidental destruction by fire of their house in March 1873: "Last night my wife and I and the foreman Photidas had the narrowest escape of being burnt alive." A letter written in April informs us that Sophia was the victim of an attempted robbery. Yet she remained with her husband until May, when she returned to Athens to bury her father.

## Rediscovery of Troy

*Trojan Antiquities,* accompanied by an *Atlas,* came out in January 1874. "This book," wrote Schliemann, "is a kind of journal of my excavations at Troy. Every section was

Sophia Schliemann gave birth to Agamemnon in 1878, seven years after the couple's firstborn, Andromache. Reciting lines from the *Iliad,* the proud father pressed Homer's epic against the newborn infant's forehead. On the christening day, it is said—to the fury of the officiating Orthodox priest—Schliemann measured the temperature of the holy water!

written by me on the spot as our work progressed." The book was essentially a reprinting of the articles he regularly dispatched to the *Times* in London. Schliemann had a flair for communication and for argument and used the press to fan the interest sparked by his archaeological investigations. But there were major obstacles to his research in the field. He did not obtain official permission to excavate until September 1871, after three trips to Constantinople and thanks to the generous intervention of an American diplomat. Nothing could be taken for granted. The following year Schliemann was informed that his previously negotiated right to keep half his finds was being withdrawn.

The first campaign began on 11 October 1871 and was a disaster. Torrential downpours brought work to a stop at the beginning of November. Schliemann's initial staff and supplies were ludicrously small. The first day he hired eight laborers. The next day there were thirty-five, and from then on they averaged eighty. They had to remove debris in baskets. Schliemann possessed only eight wheelbarrows and four bull-drawn carts. Eager to

Marking the progress of the Trojan digs (preceding pages and below), the *Illustrated London News* published a series of engravings based on watercolors by William Simpson, the magazine's correspondent on the spot. Clearly visible as it emerges from the rubble is the steeply sloping paved road, more than twenty feet wide, which led to the southwest entrance of the prehistoric citadel. Two pages from Schliemann's working notebook (opposite above) contain the archaeologist's sketches and written record of his daily finds, including ceramic pitchers like that shown opposite below.

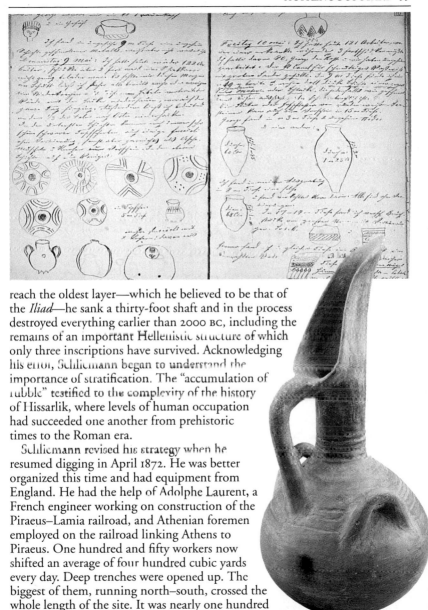

reach the oldest layer—which he believed to be that of the *Iliad*—he sank a thirty-foot shaft and in the process destroyed everything earlier than 2000 BC, including the remains of an important Hellenistic structure of which only three inscriptions have survived. Acknowledging his error, Schliemann began to understand the importance of stratification. The "accumulation of rubble" testified to the complexity of the history of Hissarlik, where levels of human occupation had succeeded one another from prehistoric times to the Roman era.

Schliemann revised his strategy when he resumed digging in April 1872. He was better organized this time and had equipment from England. He had the help of Adolphe Laurent, a French engineer working on construction of the Piraeus–Lamia railroad, and Athenian foremen employed on the railroad linking Athens to Piraeus. One hundred and fifty workers now shifted an average of four hundred cubic yards every day. Deep trenches were opened up. The biggest of them, running north–south, crossed the whole length of the site. It was nearly one hundred

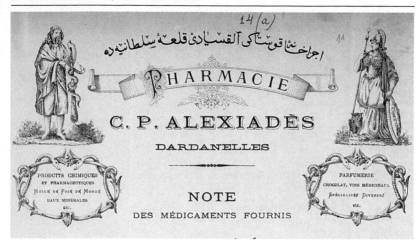

14 (a)

11

اجزا خانه قوتتكی آلقسطنطینیادی قلعه سیلطانیه ده

# PHARMACIE
## C. P. ALEXIADÈS
### DARDANELLES

PRODUITS CHIMIQUES
ET PHARMACEUTIQUES
HUILE DE FOIE DE MORUE
EAUX MINÉRALES
etc.

PARFUMERIE
CHOCOLAT, VINS MÉDICINAUX
SPÉCIALITÉS DIVERSES
etc.

### NOTE
DES MÉDICAMENTS FOURNIS

and thirty feet wide and over fifty feet deep. When malaria struck down workers on the site in mid-August, however, operations came to a halt.

But already Schliemann sensed victory. "Now, as regards the result of my excavations," he exulted, "everyone must admit that I have solved a great historical problem, and that I have solved it by the discovery of a high civilization and immense buildings upon the primary soil, in the depths of an ancient town, which throughout antiquity was called Ilium and declared itself to be the successor of Troy, the site of which was regarded as identical with the site of the Homeric Ilium by the whole civilized world of that time." For the archaeologist this triumphant report was vindicated on several grounds. Hissarlik's location corresponded to that of King Priam's citadel in the *Iliad*. A section of wall that Schliemann had uncovered might well be linked to the fortifications built at Ilium by Lysimachus, a lieutenant of Alexander the Great and later king of Thrace—but not to Priam. Finally, the confusion of foundations and walls guaranteed the existence at Hissarlik of at least three prehistoric levels. At this point Schliemann identified the deepest of them as being from the period of the Trojan War, which ancient historians dated to around 1250 BC.

The decoration of certain articles of pottery

Sickness was a permanent threat on the work site. Schliemann regularly swallowed quinine powder to prevent malaria. Above: Prescription from a Dardanelles pharmacy. Below: A Trojan vase with vaguely human features.

intrigued the excavator, leading him to a series of mistaken hypotheses. Some decorative motifs appeared to him to be the signs of a Trojan alphabet. He also developed theories about a series of anthropomorphic vases, seeing in them "the Ilian Minerva crowned with an owl's head and surmounted by a kind of helmet." He believed that a two-handled drinking cup he found illustrated a type of jug celebrated in the *Iliad*—the *depas amphikypellon.* But his readiness to see proof of the truth of the Homeric poems in every object he unearthed led Schliemann astray. Today the vessel in question is dated considerably earlier, between 2600 and 1800 BC.

While a demanding taskmaster on the site, Schliemann showed great concern for his workers' health. Appointing himself makeshift medical officer, he administered quinine, rubbed herbal ointments into cuts, and prescribed sea-bathing for a range of ailments. And in his conduct over the architectural fragment known as the "Sun Metope," the major find of 1872, he proved as determined to protect his own interests as to

Sophia and Heinrich can be seen wandering through the site in the watercolor below. "I am most anxious that local Christians or Turks be prevented from stealing the paving-stones from the tower road. To that end, I have spread the rumor that Jesus Christ visited King Priam, approaching the monarch along this very road; and to lend this story greater weight I have set a large picture of Christ in the earthen wall on the northwestern side of the tower road."

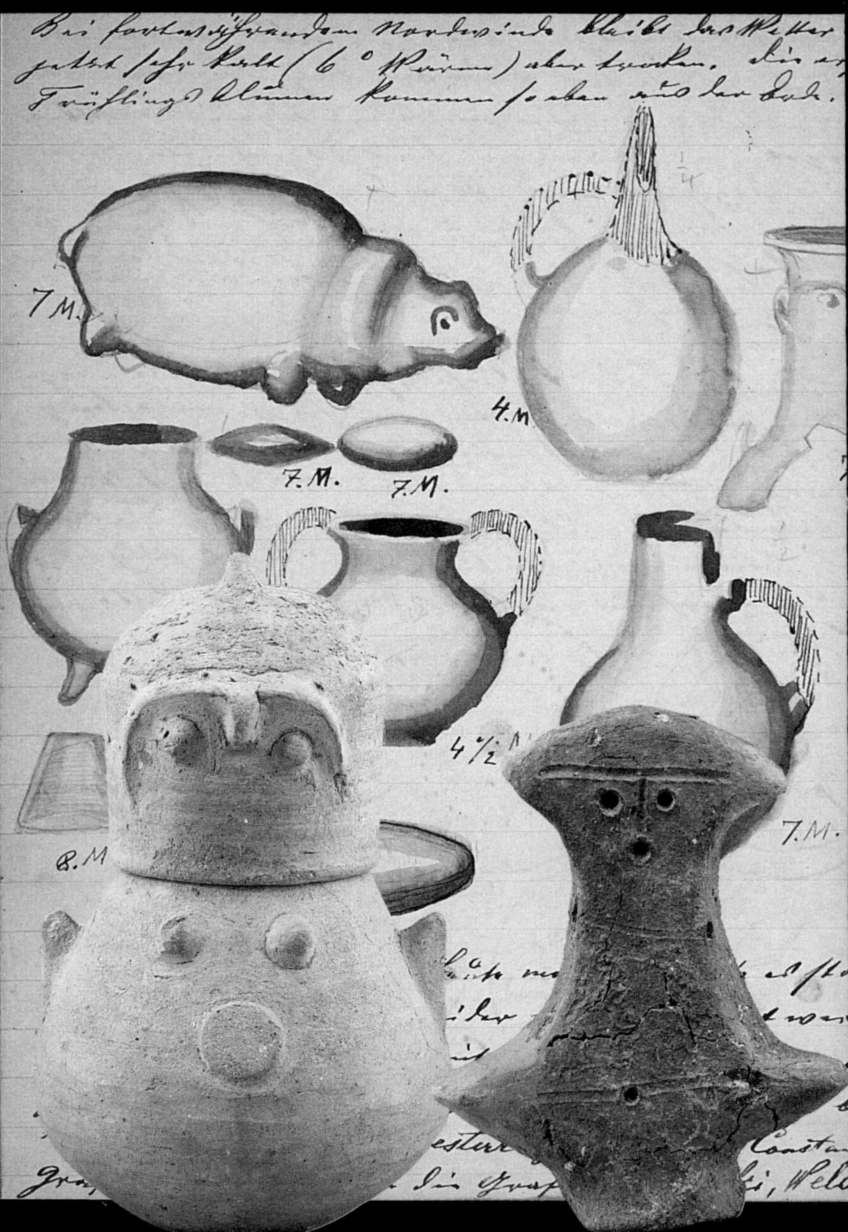
7 M.
4.M
7.M.
7.M.
4½ M
8.M
7.M.

### A Passion for Artifacts

Left and overleaf:
Schliemann's
excavation report reveals
his passion for pottery
of all kinds—vases,
terracotta articles,
earthenware—and a
fascination with
inscriptions. Objects
from left to right are
superimposed on
Schliemann's working
notes (which he made
in several different
languages). The female
form at the left is a shape
characteristic of Troy
II–V levels (2500–1800
BC). The idol in the
center is from Troy I
(3000–2500 BC). The pig
was unearthed in the
layers of Troy VI–VII
(1800–1100 BC). Overleaf,
left to right, are: a three-
legged draining jug
with handle; a *depas
amphikypellon* or two-
handled drinking cup;
a vase with tall neck,
spherical body, and
incised geometric design;
and a *pyxis*, or box with
lid. These pieces were
found in Troy II–V levels.

ΣΑ
ΕΣΑΙ                          ΟΥ
ΑΒΟΥΚΟΑ                       ΕΡΡΑΝΦ

ΣΚΑΤΑΠΛΗΘΟΣΕΙΣΟΙΝ ΣΥΡΑ
ΤΩΝ ΕΥΗ ΙΣΘΑΙΣ ΚΑΔΡΕΙΣΟ
ΙΑΝΔΡΑΣ ΤΟΥΣΣΥΝΟΘΗΣΟΜΕΝ
Ε.ΡΟΝ ΥΠΗΡ ΔΕΝ ΚΑΙ ΣΤΗΔΩΝ
ΕΝ ΤΩΙ ΤΩΝ ΣΑΜΟΘΡΑΚ
ΣΑΠΟΚΑΟΙΣ ΤΑ ΜΕΝ
ϹΝΟΥΣ ΤΗΝ ΣΥΝΘΕΣΙΝ
ΜΟΛΟΓΙΑΣ ΤΟΣΑΝΤΙΓΓΑ
ΟΙΚΗΣΟΝΤΕΣ Η.ΡΕΟΝ ΗΣ
ΟΠΕΙΘΟΥΜΙΛΗΣΙΟ
ΘΟΥΔΙΟΠΕΙΔΗΣΒ
ΤΙΦΑΝΡΙΣΑΣΤ

... im Dorf Jenischehir u. Kalifatli, ...



Topf ½ grösse

Schale ½ grösse

4. M.

7. M.

M.

6 M.

5.

M.

hold down the rising price of wine and his soaring expenses. The *metope*—a sculpted panel—from the Temple of Athena, which had dominated Ilium during the Hellenistic period, was found in the area of Hissarlik owned by Frank Calvert. Calvert had authorized Schliemann to dig there on condition that they share the objects unearthed. When they discussed the details of a future division of the spoils, Schliemann proposed simply paying his colleague and friend for what he found. After much haggling he undertook to pay Calvert one thousand francs (about two hundred dollars) for the *metope*—a fraction of Calvert's original asking price. Calvert at last wearily gave in, but when he later learned that Schliemann was quoting the value of the

"Helios here, so to speak, burst forth from the gate of day and sheds the light of his glory overall," Schliemann wrote of his spectacular find below. The "Sun Metope" belonged to the Temple of Athena. This Doric structure, probably built at the time of the Greek ruler Lysimachus (c. 355–281 BC), was adorned with a sculptured frieze on which triglyphs and *metopes* alternated. The themes they depicted may have echoed those of the Athenian Parthenon —the battles of the gods of Olympus and the sack of Troy.

*metope* at one hundred and fifty times what he had paid, Calvert rebelled and demanded compensation. Schliemann refused—on principle! "A bargain is sacred," he said. "One does not go back on it or change it: such is the world's custom."

## The "Treasure of Priam"

Schliemann's third campaign lasted from February to June of 1873. He was in a self-critical mood, regretting the destruction he had caused in sacrificing more recent structures on the Hissarlik site. He realized that he had been mistaken in assuming that Troy was built on virgin soil—as if it had known no history prior to the Greek expedition. The yield from the earliest prehistoric layer was too skimpy to have been Homeric Troy. The second stratum reflected a more advanced civilization. Its remains were impressive: a fortress some 325 feet in diameter, with dwellings inside the perimeter. Within a few weeks Schliemann cleared a gate and part of the defensive walls of this second settlement. To his Homer-obsessed way of thinking, he had discovered the Scaean Gate—the entranceway to Troy—and he decided that the domestic structures within them were the remains of the palace of the *Iliad's* Trojan ruler, Priam.

He likewise gave the two hundred and fifty gold objects he found there the collective name of the

Reproduction of the golden pin found by Schliemann in the northwestern trench, under the great Hellenic wall attributed to Lysimachus. The engraving above shows the progress of digging in May 1873. *Iliad* in hand, Schliemann identified the remains as the Palace of Priam, northwest of Troy's Scaean Gate. At the top of the mound, from left to right, are the archaeologist's wooden house, his workshop, and a stone house. Behind lie the Trojan plain and Hellespont, today's Dardanelles.

VII

VI

V

IV

III

II

I

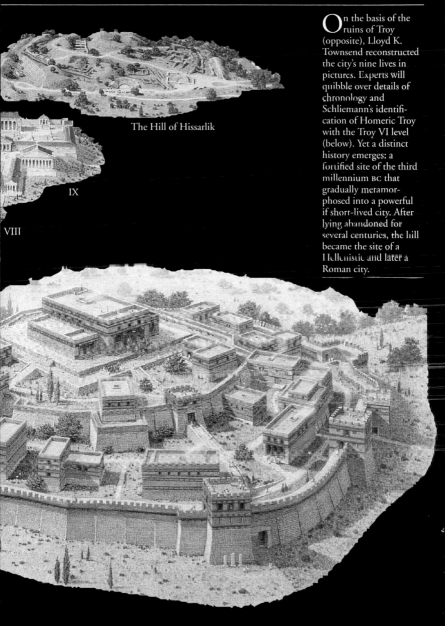

The Hill of Hissarlik

IX

VIII

On the basis of the ruins of Troy (opposite), Lloyd K. Townsend reconstructed the city's nine lives in pictures. Experts will quibble over details of chronology and Schliemann's identification of Homeric Troy with the Troy VI level (below). Yet a distinct history emerges: a fortified site of the third millennium BC that gradually metamorphosed into a powerful if short-lived city. After lying abandoned for several centuries, the hill became the site of a Hellenistic and later a Roman city.

"Treasure of Priam." The clandestine transfer to Greece of these jewels and vases raised a storm. To avoid legal proceedings Schliemann struck a bargain with the Turkish legislature and government. In exchange for fifty thousand francs, the Turks agreed to relinquish their claim to the "Treasure of Priam." Schliemann then considered that he had met his obligations and was henceforth the owner of the objects. In Paris and Berlin, however, their authenticity was questioned. So much blatant publicity had made archaeologists suspicious of this man, decidedly not one of their own. But in England a number of scientific societies invited Schliemann to address them—which pleased him immensely. In the presence of Prime Minister William Gladstone, Schliemann and his wife became honorary members of the Society of Antiquaries in Burlington House. In December 1877 he displayed the "Treasure of Priam" in London.

The exhibition was a great success. But it soon appeared that Schliemann dated his finds incorrectly. Far from being contemporary with the presumed date of the fall of Troy—around 1250 BC—they were a good millennium older, as would be demonstrated by the comparative stratigraphy (study of layers) of the Trojan and Mycenaean sites.

Even Schliemann's account of the discovery of the "Treasure of Priam" at the end of May or in mid-June 1873 carries a whiff of deceit. He tells us that at great danger to himself (the wall under which he was digging threatened to collapse and bury him at any moment), he used a knife to dislodge precious objects, gold, and jewelry. He had taken care to move his workers out of harm's way, allowing them an extra rest period. He then relied on the help of his "dear wife," constantly ready to wrap the booty in her shawl and move it to safety. Untrue. An exchange of letters

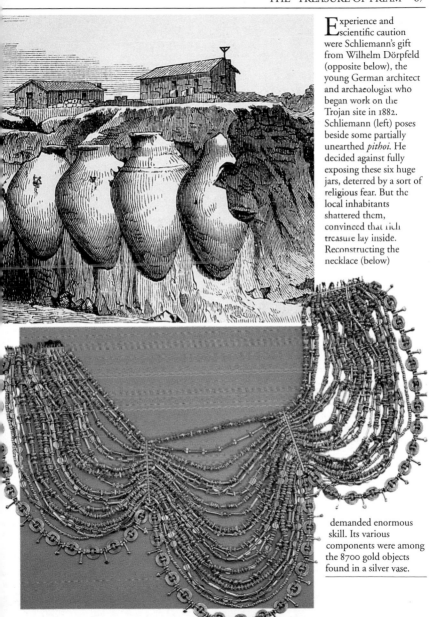

Experience and scientific caution were Schliemann's gift from Wilhelm Dörpfeld (opposite below), the young German architect and archaeologist who began work on the Trojan site in 1882. Schliemann (left) poses beside some partially unearthed *pithoi*. He decided against fully exposing these six huge jars, deterred by a sort of religious fear. But the local inhabitants shattered them, convinced that rich treasure lay inside. Reconstructing the necklace (below) demanded enormous skill. Its various components were among the 8700 gold objects found in a silver vase.

This plate from the *Atlas of Trojan Antiquities* represents what was for Schliemann one of the most interesting vases that he found: "It is a glistening red and baked right through. Its base is pointed and is here buttressed by pebbles, which hold it upright to be photographed. The crown-shaped lid was found near the vase and may have been part of it." Above: Reproduction of a brooch from the "Treasure of Priam."

shows that Sophia was not present at the time her husband says the discovery occurred. And when exactly did it take place? Intent on blurring his trail, Schliemann inevitably contradicts himself in his various excavation reports. The passage in his diary relating to the treasure is dated 17 June—"in Athens." Schliemann later falsified this, substituting "Troy" for "Athens." Other clues have lead some to believe that the "Treasure of Priam" might in fact be forgeries or a miscellaneous grab bag thrown together from a series of finds made at different areas of the site throughout the months of March and April 1873. But these theories have yet to be proved.

Anxious for the support of a scientist of unquestionable qualifications, in 1882 Schliemann hired—for a generous salary—a young architect and archaeologist, Wilhelm Dörpfeld. He had known the twenty-nine-year-old German for several years and admired his talents as a draftsman. In 1876 Dörpfeld had illustrated an article on the royal necropolis of Mycenae for a colleague of Schliemann's. The reputation of the technical director of the digs at Olympia, first undertaken in 1875, was now an accomplished fact and Dörpfeld's organizational skills and rigorous approach were widely known. Schliemann had earlier criticized Dörpfeld's painstaking level-by-level approach to the exploration of the sanctuary at Olympia as "doing everything backwards." He felt that one should plunge immediately into the depths, "only then will one find things." But Schliemann now abandoned his earlier criticisms of Dörpfeld (who had just been named architect of the celebrated German Archaeological Institute in Athens). Willingly retreating from his past strictures, Schliemann would learn from the experience and the technique of the younger man. Thanks to Dörpfeld, he realized that the archaeologist is something more than a seeker of gold.

Interior of the prehistoric citadel (foreground) and its southeast entrance, as depicted in *Ilios: the City and Country of the Trojans* (below). The wheelbarrow at right sits on a lintel of the gate. In front of the man taking notes can be seen the transverse walls and gateways. In the background, at a higher level, Roman *propylaea* —buildings forming an entranceway—dominate the tangle of structures.

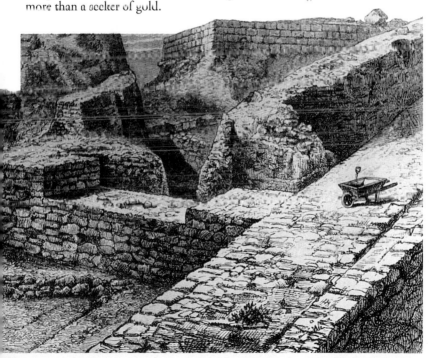

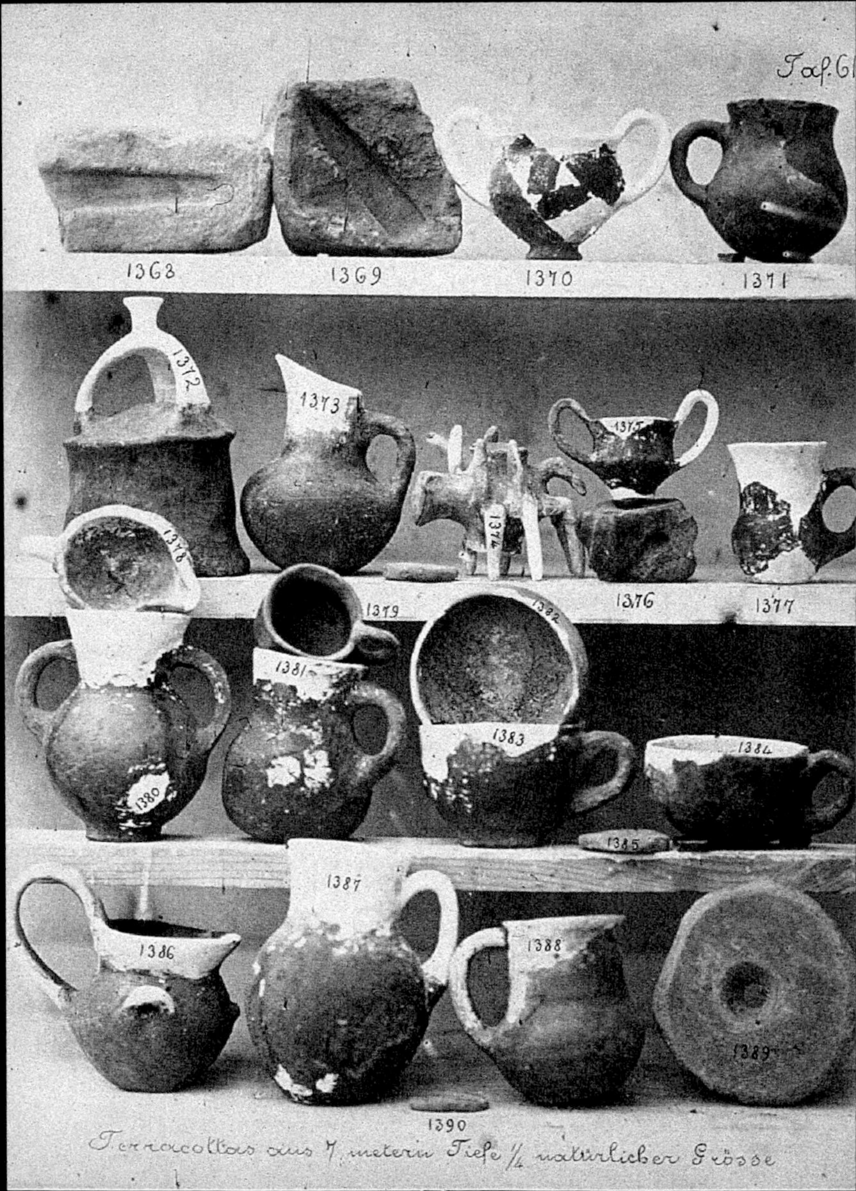
Taf. 61
1368
1369
1370
1371
1372
1373
1374
1375
1376
1377
1378
1379
1380
1381
1382
1383
1384
1385
1386
1387
1388
1389
1390
Terracottas aus 7 metern Tiefe 1/4 natürlicher Grösse

Taf. 34

834  835  836  837  838  839  840

841  842  843  844

845  846 847 848 849 850  851  852  853  854

856  857  858 859 860 861 862  863  864  865

866  867  868  869

Verschiedene Gegenstände aus 1 und 2 metern Tiefe ¼ natürlicher Grösse.

## Mycenae and the Bronze Age Warriors

In February 1874 Schliemann began excavations at
Mycenae. A century earlier a French diplomat, Louis-
François-Sébastien Fauvel, had described one of the
beehive tombs outside the citadel (largely emptied of its
contents by pillagers in ancient times). Even before the
English artist and traveler Edward Dodwell, he had
sketched the Lion Gate outside the acropolis at Mycenae.
In 1840 the newly formed Greek Archaeological Society
had begun to clear the gateway guarding the entrance.

Once again Schliemann's intuition was guided by a
reading of the ancient texts. Taking at face value the
Homeric description óf "Mycenae rich in gold," he
followed in Agamemnon's footsteps. He re-read the
"travel guide" written by the 2nd-century Greek
geographer Pausanias, who had visited the region in
search of its bygone grandeur. One of Pausanias's
passages on the funeral monuments of those heroic
times had long kindled Schliemann's interest. Already in
1869, in *Ithaca, the Peloponnese, Troy,* Schliemann had
suggested a revolutionary interpretation of the passage.
It led him to seek the royal tombs inside the perimeter of
the Mycenae acropolis, not outside. Philologists treated
him with sarcasm and accused him of being illogical.
The *Times* in London was equally amused, asserting that
"no one will find tombs within the citadel walls, unless

Previous spread: Pages
from the *Atlas of
Trojan Antiquities.*
Clearing the Lion Gate
at Mycenae (above)
of rubble put the
monument at great risk.
Somewhat rashly,
Schliemann complained
of the sluggishness of the
Greek Archaeological
Society, which had failed
to send an engineer to
shore up the various
structures. Left: English
traveler Edward
Dodwell's view of the
beehive interior of the
"Treasury of Atreus."

PAVSANIAE VE
TERIS GRAECIAE
DESCRIPTIO.

Romulus Amasæus vertit.

Accessit rerum in hisce libris
memorabilium locupletissimus index.

L. Torrentinus Ducalis Typographus excudebat.
FLORENTIAE.    M D L I.

the man who destroyed Troy dug graves there under cover of night." Nor were the Greek newspapers indulgent toward the adventurer who was poisoning their country's already difficult relations with the Ottoman Empire. They called on the authorities to rein in this ambitious man, widely suspected of being a forger. The relevant Greek government ministry grew anxious. It ordered the prefect of Nauplia, just south of Mycenae, to keep his eye on the work; then it called off Schliemann's operations entirely.

They resumed only after two years of bargaining. Schliemann appealed to all his friends, from Prime Minister Gladstone to Sophia's uncle (and their matchmaker), now archbishop of Mantinea, and from Emile Burnouf, director of the French School at Athens, to the increasingly numerous Greek archaeologists who supported his cause. Schliemann had offered the Greek

Greek geographer Pausanias's *Description of Greece* (above, title page of a 1551 Florentine edition) served, like the *Iliad* on Hissarlik, as Schliemann's guide to the discovery of Mycenae. Pausanias had himself visited Mycenae at the height of Roman imperial power. Here again, the archaeologist sought to equate the monuments he unearthed with a great text from antiquity.

Archaeological Society money to pay for the demolition of the Frankish Tower—symbol of Turkish occupation—on the Acropolis. This gesture of support for Greek freedom helped secure official permission to resume digging. With a hundred laborers, the excavations lasted from August to December 1876.

The operation was carried out under the auspices of the Greek Archaeological Society and the direction of a young Greek archaeologist, Panagiotis Stamatakis. Schliemann's relations with this representative of the host government were stormy. Each did his best to make life impossible for the other. On the site, Sophia's exchanges with her young countryman were far from cordial. Schliemann wrote his excavation reports in English to prevent Stamatakis from deciphering them. Stamatakis criticized the haphazard placing of Schliemann's digs. Schliemann was intent on locating all the monuments that Pausanias had seen and named after the heroes of the *Iliad*. To his wife he entrusted the exploration of the so-called Clytemnestra's Tomb. He explored the approaches to the "Treasury of Atreus" and sank several shafts near the Lion Gate. Both his objectives and his methods drew fire. But criticism died after the discovery of a grave circle inside the citadel. For Schliemann, the controversy over Pausanias's text seemed to be resolved. The man in the field had won out over the desk-bound scholar.

His ambition remained unchanged: to bring Homer's world back to life by fitting the texts of the epic poems—taken as historical guidelines—to the archaeological remains. When the first golden masks emerged from the five shaft graves he had uncovered, Schliemann was convinced that he held King Agamemnon's mask in his hands. "I have the greatest joy," he cabled King George I of Greece, "to announce to Your Majesty that I have discovered the tombs which tradition, transmitted by Pausanias, has designated as the tombs of Agamemnon, Cassandra, Eurymedon, and their companions, all

Plan de
L'ACROPOLE DE
AVEC LES FOUI
du
D.r HENRY SCHL
par Vasilios Dran
Lion

Metres

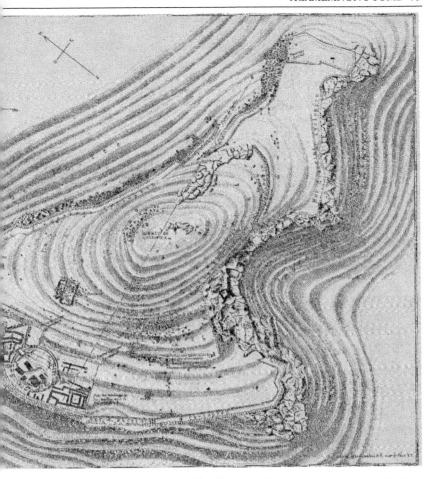

slain at table by Clytemnestra and her lover Aegisthus.... In the sepulchers I have found immense treasure in archaic objects and pure gold. By themselves alone these treasures are enough to fill a great museum, which will be the world's most wonderful and which for centuries to come will draw thousands of foreigners from all countries to Greece." In all, over thirty pounds of golden artifacts were consigned to the Bank of Greece.

These golden objects would soon be the pride of the

Inside the citadel efforts were finally focused on the grave circle (bottom left of plan). Opposite: One of the four masks found in the fourth tomb of the grave circle (16th century BC).

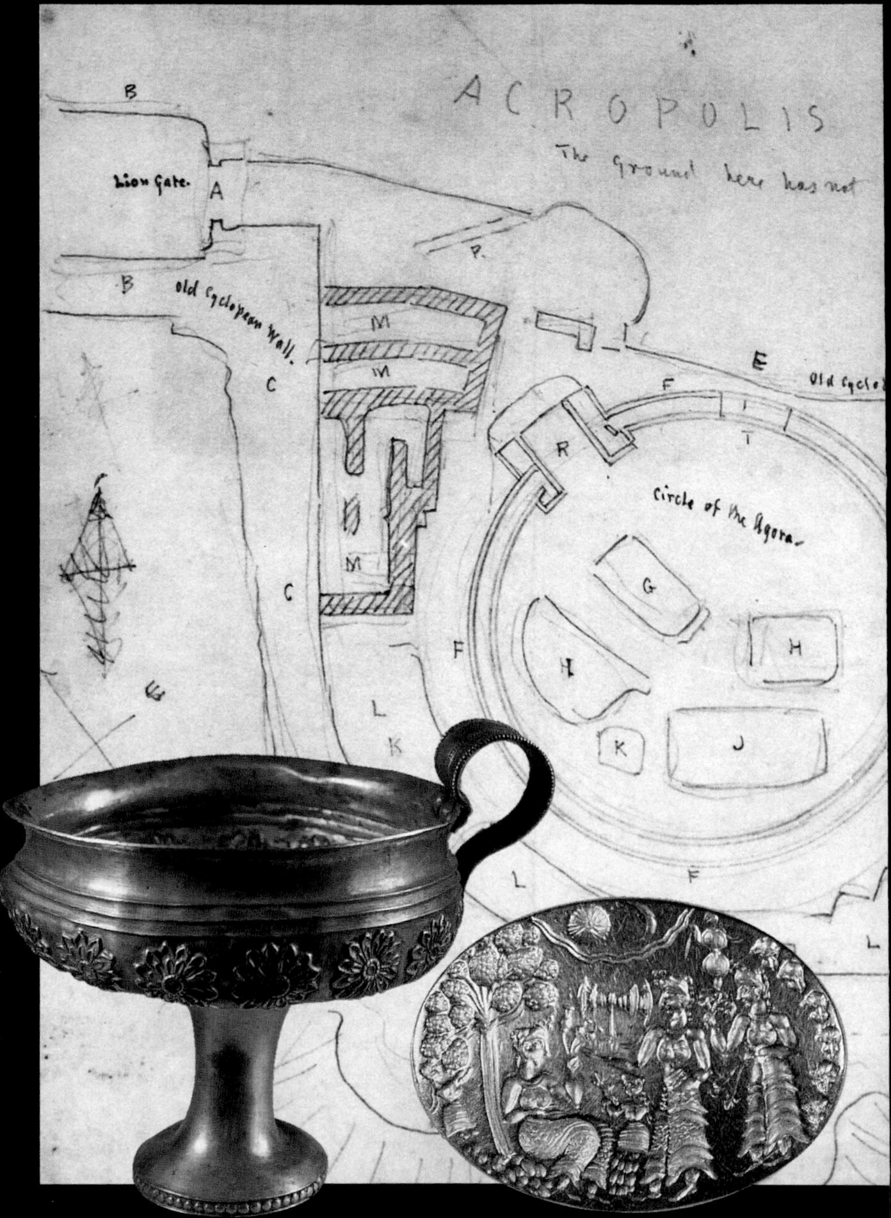

ACROPOLIS

The ground here has not

B

Lion Gate.

A

B    old cyclopean wall.

C

P.

M

M

M

M

C

E    Old cyclo

F    T

R

Circle of the Agora.

G

I

H

K    J

F

L

K

F

L

L

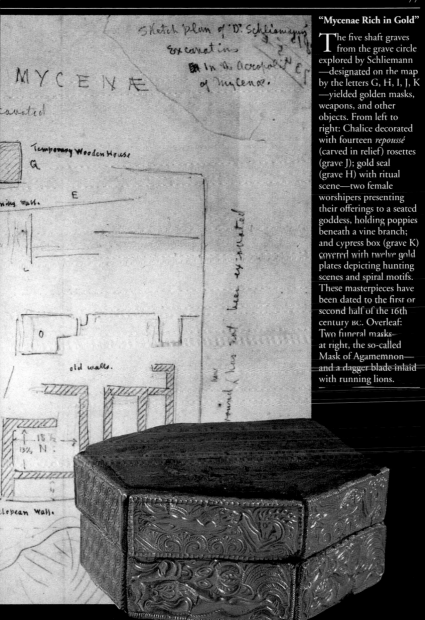

**"Mycenae Rich in Gold"**

The five shaft graves from the grave circle explored by Schliemann —designated on the map by the letters G, H, I, J, K —yielded golden masks, weapons, and other objects. From left to right: Chalice decorated with fourteen *repoussé* (carved in relief) rosettes (grave J); gold seal (grave H) with ritual scene—two female worshipers presenting their offerings to a seated goddess, holding poppies beneath a vine branch; and cypress box (grave K) covered with twelve gold plates depicting hunting scenes and spiral motifs. These masterpieces have been dated to the first or second half of the 16th century BC. Overleaf: Two funeral masks— at right, the so-called Mask of Agamemnon— and a dagger blade inlaid with running lions.

*Handwritten on sketch:*

Sketch plan of Dr Schliemann's Excavations In the Acropolis of Mycenae.

MYCENAE

...avated

Temporary Wooden House

G

E

...ning walls.

...

O

old walls.

...15 1/2...

13 1/4  N.

...lopean Wall.

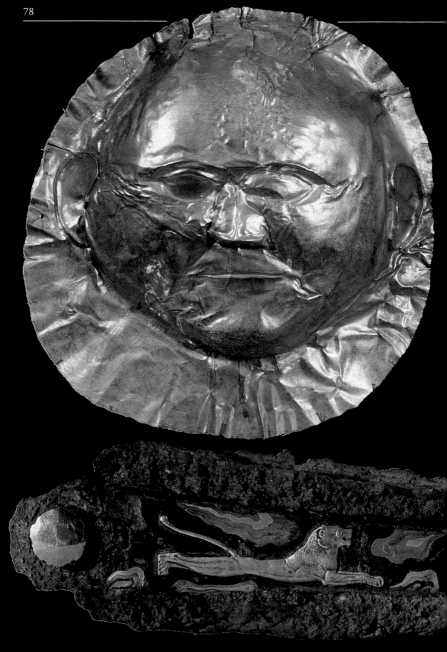

*ycenae* (opposite: the original cover) was first published in English. Schliemann used the contents of three major photo albums as the basis for the engravings illustrating the book. The British archaeologist Sinclair Hood purchased the original albums from an Athens bookseller in 1955. The photographs were the work of the Romaïdes brothers and showed the objects before restoration, just as they were found. One funeral mask was so badly crushed that it was simply a shapeless mass. Among the 296 documents found in the albums (apart from Schliemann's own notes and sketches) were original plans and watercolors reproducing monuments and discoveries. They were executed by various Schliemann collaborators, such as Vasilios Drosinos or Dimitrios V. Tountopoulos. Left: Title page of the portfolio of watercolors of Mycenae by William Simpson.

Athenian Polytechnikon, the future National Archaeological Museum. But the objects in ivory and silver and earthenware were equally spectacular. In 1882 Schliemann wrote proudly, "so great is the press of foreigners who have come to see these treasures that there are already ten times more hotels in Athens than before my excavations." Early in 1878 *Mycenae* appeared. This stout, well-illustrated volume reproduced and enlarged upon the reports sent the previous year to the London *Times*.

Although the new book was a blend of myth and fact, its author did not confine himself to the revelation of the newfound masterpieces. The book opened a new field in

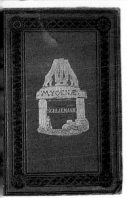

Greek studies—Mycenaean civilization. Before Schliemann Mycenae had been simply a name, its role in recorded history confined to a minor participation in the Persian Wars and destruction by Argos in 468 BC. Apart from the references in Homer and the much later tragedy by Aeschylus, almost nothing was known of the citadel in heroic times. Schliemann's excavations were an introduction to this vanished world, which had reached its apogee during the Bronze Age, between 1600 and 1125 BC. The discoveries provided a cultural model that would reappear in Argos and throughout Greece.

However, the graves unearthed by Schliemann are older than he believed. We now know, in the light of discoveries made during the 1950s, that they were in use between 1600 and 1510 BC. In the 13th century BC they were ringed by a circular structure integrated into the citadel precincts, as if Mycenae's rulers sought to emphasize their reverence for the tombs. Finally, the funeral ritual they reveal— burial —fails to correspond to the practices described by Homer, whose heroes were burned on funeral pyres after their death. In identifying the graves with the Mycenaean warriors of the Trojan War, Schliemann was wrong.

Schliemann's excavations paved the way for a new examination of the funeral customs of the Mycenaean world. The *tholoi* (beehive-shaped graves) are no longer necessarily identified as royal graves. In November 1951 a new grave circle, comparable in size to the one exhumed by Schliemann, was cleared. Older, and less rich in objects, it was in use between 1650 and 1550 BC. Thus the royal Mycenaean dynasty seems to have displaced a primitive oligarchical system. The new rulers remained attached to the aristocratic values of hunting and war, as the many weapons deposited in the graves (below, ornamental dagger) testify.

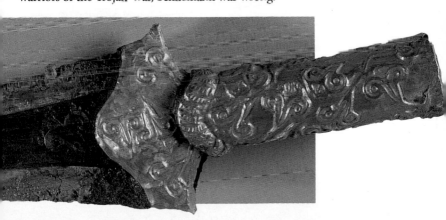

## Archaeologists Gather at the Site

After a visit to the site, the obligatory pose for the camera at the entrance of the *tholos* known as Clytemnestra's Tomb (this page). Opposite: Archaeologists gather before the Lion Gate. According to one of his biographers, Leo Deuel, Heinrich Schliemann is standing at the summit, one hand on the sculpted portal. Wilhelm Dörpfeld is on the left, above, sitting in a breach in the ramparts. On the ground, Sophia Schliemann (far right) sits on a stone block at the entrance to the citadel. Overleaf: The grave circle after Schliemann's excavations and consolidation efforts. Inset is an engraving based on Plate V of the first of the photo albums purchased by Sinclair Hood. Schliemann annotated this general view of the grave circle and of the five tombs investigated. The original photo is signed Tountopoulos

"We could describe Schliemann's excavations on the hill of Hissarlik and consider their results without speaking of Troy or even alluding to it; even then, those discoveries would retain their value; even then, they would have added a whole new chapter to the history of civilization, the history of art."

Georges Perrot
*Journal des Savants,* 1891

## CHAPTER V
# THE ARCHAEOLOGIST AS MODERN HERO

A sixty-year-old man and a thirty-year-old woman: the Schliemanns (opposite), painted by Eugene Broerrmann. Schliemann's tomb (right) in the First Cemetery of Athens.

Fresh sites beckoned the pioneer of Mycenaean archaeology: Ithaca and Orchomenos in Boeotia. But the results were less spectacular. Seeking to authenticate events recorded by history, Schliemann turned next to the battlefields where Greeks and Persians had once clashed, digging at Thermopylae in 1883 and at Marathon in 1884, but again without success. He started excavations at Tiryns but lost heart when his plans to explore Knossos collapsed. Gold had become elusive…. Schliemann then went to Central America and Cuba, followed by Egypt. He returned to Egypt with a friend who had assisted him on his last digs in the Troad, the doctor Rudolf Virchow. One last dream haunted Schliemann: discovering the tomb of Alexander the Great in the Egyptian city he had founded, Alexandria. Like the fallen king Sisyphus, who was doomed to forever roll a rock uphill, the archaeologist was tirelessly ranging the world in his quest to reawaken the past.

## The Archaeologist's Personal Palace

In 1878, returning to Ithaca with the *Odyssey* as his guide, Schliemann entrusted the architect Ernst Ziller with the task of creating for him an Athens home befitting his name and reputation. The Iliou Melathron, or House of Ilium, with its polychrome mosaics and walls decorated with frescoes glorifying Schliemann's excavations, was inaugurated two years later with a grand ball. Some dignitaries were shocked by the nakedness of the statues on the building's roof, and Schliemann playfully had them clothed in brightly colored robes. The guests then urged him to undress them. He did so himself, to the delight of the Athenians.

Wined and dined all over Europe, the gentleman-archaeologist was now at the height of his fame. He admitted to having a huge income of which he annually spent half, the bulk of it on archaeological research. In 1875 he had even explored the Isle of Motya off Sicily—in search

of a Phoenician settlement—and Alba Longa, where he sought to solve the mystery of Rome's origins. The following year he prudently refused to dig at the Etruscan city of Chiusi, since he felt that it presented no problem for him to solve, and he would find nothing there that was not already to be found in museums. Schliemann's great achievement was to have inaugurated "investigative" archaeology. He was, however, beginning to realize that the objective he had always set himself—fitting the architectural remains to the written texts—had its limits. In 1880 he investigated

For his house in Athens, Iliou Melathron (above), Schliemann hired the architect Ernst Ziller (opposite), a specialist in neoclassical construction inspired by the Italian Renaissance. Schliemann had met him ten years earlier in Athens while Ziller was taking part in excavations in the Troad. Buying furniture for his Athenian residence by catalogue (left), Schliemann was now spending money right and left.

Today hemmed in by modern buildings on noisy, polluted Venizelos Avenue, Schliemann's Athenian residence has lost much of its former charm. But the Muses still gaze down from the loggia ceiling (opposite) and the mosaic floors of the entranceway depict Mycenaean jewelry. Lines from Homer, Hesiod, and Pindar adorn the marble-covered walls in letters of gold. The ballroom, an extension of the dining room, is decorated with a large fresco (below). The bedrooms, library, and Schliemann's study were on the second floor.

the necropolis of Orchomenos, a city the *Iliad* describes as "rich in sheep" and whose "Treasure of Minyas" is mentioned by Pausanias. The dig revealed nothing spectacular; the relation of ancient tradition to the realities on the ground thus could not be taken automatically for granted.

Schliemann remained a controversial figure. Jealous of his finds academics rejected his beginnings and the unorthodox intellectual itinerary he had followed. To publicize his activities he chose the forum of popular magazines rather than specialist journals. And the attacks from academic circles were personal rather than scientific. Ulrich von Wilamowitz-Möllendorf, the leading German Hellenist of the day, heaped scorn on the Schliemanns. The retired businessman's wealth was thrown in his face; it raised suspicions about the origins of his discoveries. There was dark talk of disguised purchases or forgeries. And it was true that Schliemann exploited his fortune in the cause of his own fame, hiring journalists and scholars to write articles in his praise. This hunger for publicity undercut his prestige in the public's eyes. In 1881 Adolf Furtwängler, respected curator of the Berlin Museums, delivered this damning verdict: "Schliemann is hugely celebrated here. Nevertheless, he is and remains half-mad, a man of confused ideas who has no idea of the value of his discoveries." The explorer of Troy and Mycenae would never be admitted to the Berlin Academy—an honor

The self-educated Schliemann valued marks of distinction and intellectual recognition (above: diploma from the German Anthropological Society). In the archives of the Gennadius Library in Athens are an additional eighteen diplomas awarded the scientist by scientific institutions in Europe and the United States. Top: The site of ancient Orchomenos by Edward Dodwell.

reserved for university figures. But on 7 July 1881, with great pomp, he was awarded honorary citizenship of the city of Berlin: "By dedicating his practical activity to the service of an ideal," the award noted, "he has become a model for his fellow-citizens." Schliemann had just presented his Trojan collection, until then on display in London, to the German people. His friend Rudolf Virchow had advised that he make the move.

Schliemann and Virchow (below left) wrote one another regularly from 1876 to 1890. Their recently published correspondence is a mine of information. The London letter, dated 14 July 1884, informs Virchow about Schliemann's movements and the state of his health. The letter from Boulogne, on the north-west coast of France, is a miniature treatise on the Tiryns excavations.

THE GRAND HOTEL.
TRAFALGAR SQUARE.
LONDON,

HÔTEL
Pavillon Impérial et des Bains de Mer

VERMERSCH-DUCHOCHOIS, Propriétaire

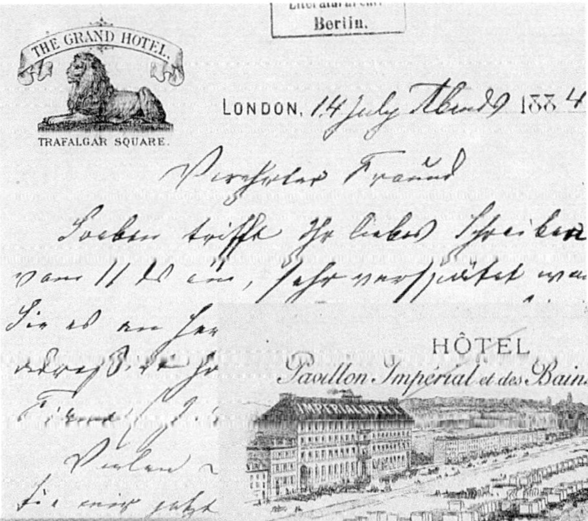

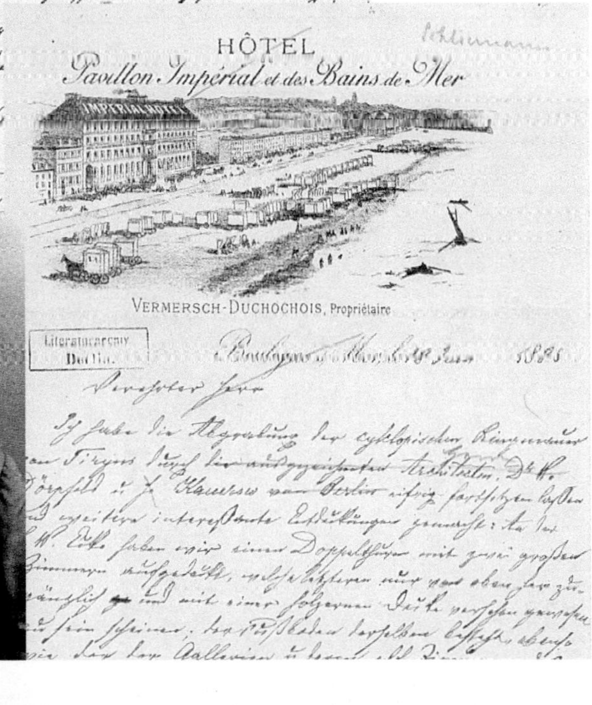

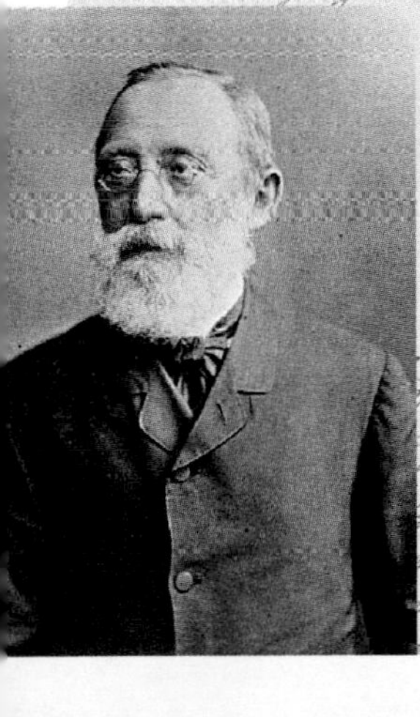

## Tiryns: The Earliest Mycenaean Palace

As early as 1876 Schliemann had looked for the Palace of Tiryns in the Argive—the area around Argos, where he sank several exploratory shafts. According to the *Iliad* Diomedes had reigned there. The master of eighty warships, Diomedes was a respected chieftain whose sway extended as far as Epidaurus and Hermione. But, absorbed by Mycenae and later by new investigations in the Troad, Schliemann would not resume work on the citadel site until March 1884.

When he did eventually return to work at Tiryns, he again joined forces with Dörpfeld, who played an important part in the investigation. Two campaigns, each lasting several weeks, laid bare the earliest example of a Mycenaean palace. For Schliemann these remains made it possible to envisage the living conditions of Homeric kings. He believed that the courtyard of the *gynechaeum*, or women's quarters, overlooked by a line of rooms, and the banquet hall in Ithaca where Penelope and her suitors met in the *Odyssey*, found a parallel here. The existence of massive fortifications lends credence to the legend that seven Cyclops—one-eyed giants—were employed to build the walls.

In 1941 the archaeologist Arne Furumark published a landmark study of Mycenaean pottery. But Schliemann had been the first archaeologist to appreciate the significance of such production (above, color plate from *Tiryns*).

Following the Mycenaean tombs, the picture of Greek princely society finally became clear with the appearance of Schliemann's new book, *Tiryns*. Published simultaneously in German, English, and French, the book was an archaeological publishing event. It reached the booksellers in November 1885, just four months after the last blows of the archaeologist's pickax, but, like the excavation itself, the book suffered from hasty execution.

An architectural overview served as preface, written by Friedrich Adler, Dörpfeld's father-in-law and former teacher. The latter, entrusted with illustrating the book, also wrote two major chapters, one on the construction and design of the palace, the other on the 1885 digs. An Asia Minor expert, Ernst Fabricius, wrote the notes for the objects unearthed during the last digging season. Schliemann himself prepared the catalogue of the most ancient finds and reconstructed the history of the site. In a brief overview he also suggested

We owe the adjective "Cyclopean," used to characterize the massive stone-block structures at Tiryns (below), to the Greek geographer Pausanias. In 1884 Schliemann and Dörpfeld cleared part of the ogive-(pointed arch) built southeastern great hall. Once again, controversy erupted. Schliemann was accused of mistaking Byzantine-era remains for a palace dating from the second millennium BC. "Schliemann's luck has deserted him," complained the *New York Times*. "He has found no gold nor any object of any value whatsoever."

the possibility of a Phoenician presence in ancient Greece and analyzed the legend of the birth of the "sun god and hero" Hercules at Tiryns.

Lacking comparative evidence, Schliemann was unable to comment on one outstanding find, but he realized its importance and had it reproduced on the cover of the book. It was a fragment of a mural depicting a man leaping onto a bull's back. Fifteen years later the British archaeologist Sir Arthur Evans would interpret it in light of the bull-jumping frescoes at Knossos. As it would later transpire, comparisons between the Homeric world and the Mycenaean palaces had little meaning, while Crete's influence on the Mycenaean world was much more obvious and decisive. Schliemann, intent on verifying Homer's reference to "the city where Minos, confidant of great Zeus, reigned in nine-year cycles," would be unlucky in Crete. As he states in one of his letters, he would have liked to "investigate the prehistoric palaces of the kings of Knossos in Crete," a project he thought would take "a week with a hundred men." This never materialized. During Schliemann's last stay at Knossos in 1889, negotiations with the site's owners failed at the eleventh hour. The owners claimed that the price they sought was justified by the presence on their

For the cover of *Tiryns* (above) Schliemann ordered a watercolor sketch (opposite) of an intriguing fresco fragment discovered near the *megaron*, or main hall. The significance of the find became apparent only when Sir Arthur Evans, in the first years of this century, unearthed a similar bull-jumping scene in the east wing of the palace at Knossos.

The design of the krater (a wide-bodied jar often used for mixing) below—depicting warriors and a hound escorting a chariot—has been gradually pieced together.

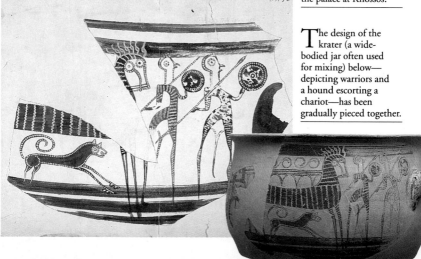

land of twenty five hundred olive trees. Schliemann counted less than nine hundred. Deciding that he had been lied to, he refused the deal. King Minos's palace slipped from his grasp; its discovery was to fall later to Sir Arthur Evans.

## Ilios: the City and Country of the Trojans

In ancient Greece the poet was known as a "rhapsode," in other words one who "stitches together" fragments of song, sometimes of diverse origins, in order to compose an original story. Schliemann used this technique in the writing of *Ilios: the City and Country of the Trojans,* which appeared in 1880. Here Schliemann was overseeing a collective enterprise, organizing and conducting the efforts of a multidisciplinary team.

Running to a thousand pages in all, and with an introduction by Virchow, the book outlined the history of the seven settlements uncovered by Schliemann at Hissarlik. Twelve appendices, drawn up by five authors, including Frank Calvert, tackled as many different themes on Troy and its surroundings: ancient inscriptions, relations with Egypt, the role of metals in the prehistoric era, Hera Boöpis and the cattle cult, Hellenistic Ilium, and contemporary medical practices. The book, combining letters, reports, and analyses, is an astonishingly modern apologia for a scientifically based archaeology, calling on experts from many fields:

*Tiryns* pays tribute to Kikolaos Yannakis, Schliemann's loyal foreman on Hissarlik who was accidentally drowned in 1883. The excavation (like the book that resulted from it) was a team effort. Another fruit of this collective editorial endeavor was *Ilios: the City and Country of the Trojans.* Unusually for a scientific work, it began with the principal author's autobiography, which explained how the exploration of Troy was the fulfillment of a childhood dream. In his conclusion, Schliemann reported his financial holdings. Responding to detractors who accused him of squandering his money, Schliemann reassured them that a family man would never dream of ruining his children through archaeological follies. "My excavations do not cost me more than 125,000 francs per year; so that every year I am able to increase my capital by a sum equivalent to my expenses. I thus hope to leave to my children a fortune which will permit them to continue their father's scientific activities without eating into their capital."

epigraphy, ceramics, geography, geology, botany, chemistry, and medicine.

The archaeologist was still seized with a passion for business. Worried by the imminent prospect of the liberation of slaves in Cuba, he went there in 1886 to look after his sugarcane estates. Still on business, he visited Paris, Berlin, and then London. At a meeting of the Hellenic Society on 3 July he took the opportunity to answer those who accused him of burying the ancient wall of Tiryns beneath the debris of his excavation, and of misjudging the antiquity of the site. Dörpfeld was present. The two men were able to convince their listeners.

Heinrich and Sophia (left) adding the finishing touches to displays at the opening of the Trojan exhibition in Berlin in 1881. Schliemann (who with German Chancellor Otto von Bismarck and the military strategist Helmut von Moltke was one of the rare honorary citizens of the city) commented: "I am prey to varied emotions. Today is perhaps but a semicolon in one paragraph of my life. Yes, this is true, and this thought comforts me in the tumult of recent events." Schliemann (above) would soon be off to Egypt.

Named for its handle and fitted with a narrow spout, the stirrup vase (below), was the most typical of Mycenaean pottery forms. Schliemann realized early on the value —from a chronological standpoint—of evidence unearthed in Egypt. When found alongside funeral material in clearly defined physical contexts, such objects provided a key for precise dating. Schliemann discovered this drawing of four Mycenaean stirrup vases (above) in the tomb of Ramses III in Egypt.

## Egyptian Mirage

Schliemann was surprisingly self-effacing as a patron of the arts. He did not attend the opening on 18 December 1886 of the Trojan Rooms at the new Berlin Ethnological Museum. For the past month he had been on a solo cruise up the Nile to Luxor. Schliemann was dreaming of Cleopatra and of Alexander. He was also studying the question of lighting in the Pharaonic temples. He collected pottery shards and stone objects. Above all he sought points of convergence between the Aegean world and Egyptian civilization. A stirrup-handled Mycenaean vase depicted on a wall of Ramses III's tomb caught his attention. It was similar to those he had uncovered in Argos—which meant he could now date those objects with great accuracy: for Ramses III was known to have reigned from 1198 to 1166 BC.

In 1887 Schliemann received permission to dig at Pylos in the Peloponnese, where he now hoped to bring to light the palace of Nestor, king of Pylos, according to Homer. But that winter he returned to Egypt. In February 1888 he excavated a few steps of a great staircase and the foundations of a palace in Alexandria. Against all the laws of probability, Schliemann was determined to believe that this could only be Cleopatra's palace! His single-mindedness drove him to falsify information. He exhibited a marble portrait said to be of the Egyptian queen, but he produced no proof that he had actually found it there; in fact, he probably purchased it. We know today that this Roman copy of a Greek original represents Corinna, rival of the 5th-century BC poet Pindar—not

the mistress of Pompey and Caesar.

Schliemann then returned to the Nile, where Virchow joined him. Schliemann was disappointed to not be able to proceed with the excavations he had planned near the Nebit Daniil Mosque in Cairo in hopes of finding Alexander the Great's tomb. He returned to Athens after learning that a Mycenaean stirrup-handled vase had been found in a Fayum grave in Lower Egypt dating back even earlier than the previous vases to the years 1304–1237 BC, the reign of Ramses II. He was convinced that Egyptian soil would give the dedicated seeker the answers to the riddles of Greece. The pharaohs' dates provided a sound chronological framework for the Greek objects found buried in their graves. Comparative archaeology was emerging.

Bötticher's book on Hissarlik (above). Left: Fascinated as ever by death, Schliemann sent Virchow this photo from Egypt of a mummified head that had intrigued him.

## Return to Troy

But first Schliemann's detractors had to be confronted. One of them, Ernst Bötticher, a retired artillery officer, was publishing books and pamphlets to prove—on the basis of material gathered during excavations—that the structures on the hill of Hissarlik had been designed for an exclusively funerary purpose. Bötticher's thesis was well received at the International Congress of Anthropology held in Paris in the summer of 1889. It was developed further by Salomon Reinach—a former member of the French School at Athens, a member of the Académie Française, and curator of the Museum of Saint-Germain-en-Laye outside Paris—in his article "Chronique d'Orient" ("A Tale of the East") in the magazine *Revue Archéologique*. Schliemann fought back. To win the scientifically minded public to his cause, he hired a university professor, Carl Schuchhardt, to write the history of his excavations and discoveries. The book was published in Leipzig in 1891. To confound his adversaries in the field, Schliemann then convened the first of two conferences in Troy itself. In December 1889, with Dörpfeld at his side, he welcomed Bötticher to Hissarlik. He also invited,

as witnesses, Georg Niemann, a professor of the Viennese Academy of Fine Arts, and Bernhard Steffen, an officer on the king of Prussia's staff who had published plans and maps of Mycenae. Bötticher departed unconvinced; the two witnesses were converts to Schliemann's cause even before their arrival.

But the conference had a positive result: The Turkish government granted Schliemann fresh authorization to dig. Work resumed on 1 March 1890. A second Trojan conference also brought a number of experts together. Their observations and work confirmed their host's own conclusions. Meanwhile, there was great amusement abroad over "Schliemannopolis"—the barracks that their host had built to house them for the occasion.

On the work site (where small carts were now being used to haul out the rubble) there was a double objective. The first was to lay bare the remains of the second prehistoric settlement on Hissarlik, known as Troy II. This—among the seven successive Troys identified by

Under the leadership of Schliemann and Dörpfeld, new excavations began at Hissarlik in March 1890. Several witnesses were invited to the conference convened by Schliemann to mark the occasion (below, posing for the official photo). Behind Frank Calvert (seated, front row left) stands Schliemann. On his right are Wilhelm Grempler and Virchow. The conference issued a declaration in support of Schliemann's opinions against the positions sustained by Bötticher.

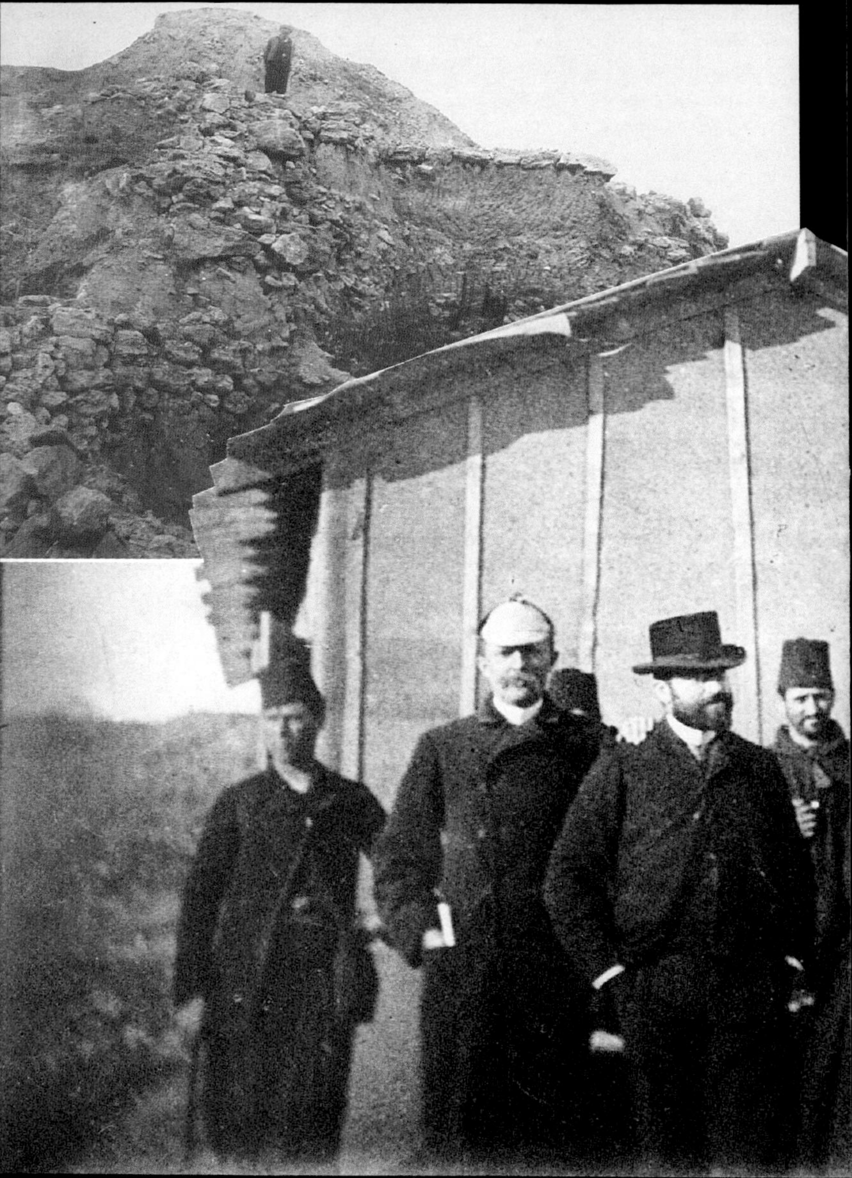

$S$chliemann welcomed
Major Bernhard
Steffen to Troy in
1889 (above). The
archaeologists invited
to the second Trojan
conference, in 1890, were
housed on the site, in
the barracks erected at
"Schliemannopolis"
as Georges Perrot called
it. The photo at left,
captioned by Virchow,
includes "Zaptieh [in
deerstalker], Dörpfeld,
Mr. Babin, Scherkasse
[in fez], Mrs. Babin,
Telamon, Schliemann,
Christophoros, and
Ghalib Effendi."

the digs and numbered in ascending order from the oldest to the most recent—was the level that Schliemann believed to be the Homeric city. The second objective was to begin new digs outside the ramparts of Troy II. Schliemann exhumed a marble head he took to be that of Emperor Caligula in the Roman levels of the excavation. It fell to Dörpfeld to make a major discovery: the foundations of a rectangular hall with a centrally placed hearth. Pottery fragments linked to this structure were comparable to those found in the Mycenaean shaft graves. This level also revealed a new prehistoric site,

## Troy's Nine Lives

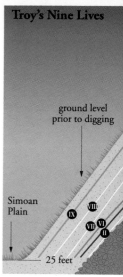

ground level prior to digging

Simoan Plain

25 feet

Dörpfeld continued Schliemann's excavations after 1893 (left and overleaf, his Trojan excavations of 1894). By the end of his investigations Dörpfeld had identified nine levels of occupation. In his view, Homer's Troy was Troy VI. Like Herodotus he located its fall around 1250 BC— a date disputed since antiquity. Eratosthenes, director of the Alexandria library in the 2nd century BC, believed it happened in about 1150 BC.

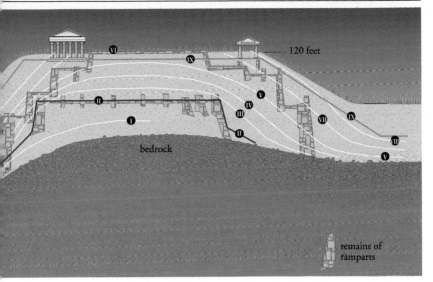

designated Troy VI. For Dörpfeld this complex—much bigger than its predecessors and heavily fortified—was the city celebrated in the *Iliad*.

At this point (in 1890) Dörpfeld did not yet know the full extent of Troy VI, where he began excavation after Schliemann's departure. But he had already managed to date this sixth level, and thus undermine his friend Schliemann's earlier theories. The "Treasure of Priam" (in Troy) and "Mask of Agamemnon" (at Mycenae) were not contemporaneous, as Schliemann had believed. A thousand years separated them. Indeed, a kind of pottery present only in the sixth Trojan layer and in the Mycenaean sepulchers proved that Troy VI was contemporaneous with the grave circle at Mycenae. The much older Troy II (the Troy of the "Treasure of Priam") could not be the city where Helen had dwelt and Odysseus and his companions slaughtered and plundered during the Trojan War.

It cost Schliemann dear but he acknowledged his mistake, even stressing it in the conclusion of his last report. Urged by Dörpfeld to reexamine the whole Homeric question, he planned to undertake a new investigation. On 22 July he wrote to Prince Otto von

Troy I: a fortified site, 3000–2500 BC. Troy II: 2500–2200 (it was at this level that Schliemann found the "Treasure of Priam"). Troy III: 2200–2050. Troy IV: 2050–1900. Troy V: 1900–1800. Troy VI (1800–1300): To Dörpfeld this was Homer's city, although it was destroyed by an earthquake. Troy VII (1300–1000): a city ravaged by a violent fire, repopulated by the survivors, perhaps invaded around 1200, then abandoned. Troy VIII: reoccupation around 700 BC. Troy IX: Hellenistic and Roman city.

When he discovered the imposing remains of Troy VI (left, view of the northeast tower), Wilhelm Dörpfeld, director of the German Archaeological Institute in Athens, thought he had stumbled upon confirmation of Schliemann's brilliant intuition. Below: Dörpfeld lightheartedly posing neck-deep in a huge storage jar.

Bismarck: "My workers and I are utterly exhausted. I shall be forced to suspend operations on August 1. But if Heaven grants me life I intend to resume work with all the energy at my disposal on 1 March 1891." Death would thwart his plans.

## Schliemann's Legacy

Schliemann had long suffered from an earache, which became unbearable in the autumn of 1890. Virchow

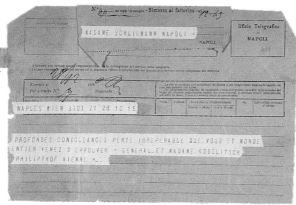

Schliemann's body was taken from Naples to Athens by Dörpfeld and by Sophia's elder brother. At her husband's death, Sophia received countless expressions of sympathy (left). One of the first to offer tribute and condolences was German Emperor Wilhelm II. The funeral took place in the afternoon of 4 January 1891 in the presence of King George I of Greece, the Greek prime minister, the United States ambassador, and a host of Greek and foreign scientists. A huge crowd joined the procession. Dörpfeld read his friend's funeral eulogy. It ended with these words: "Rest in peace. You have done enough."

made him promise to consult a specialist in Germany. In early November he went to Halle, where Dr. Hermann Schwartz examined him and decided to operate. As soon as he was dismissed from the clinic, Schliemann left for Leipzig to confer with his publisher; in December he journeyed to Paris. But the pains persisted and grew worse. Now deaf, Schliemann decided to return to Greece. He stopped en route in Naples, intending to see Pompeii again. On Christmas Day he collapsed, comatose, on a street near the Piazza Carità. On 26 December 1890 he died at the Grand Hotel in Naples, without emerging from his coma. He was buried in Athens at a funeral attended by throngs of onlookers on 4 January 1891.

Troy continued to baffle experts even after the archaeologist's death. Dörpfeld carried on Schliemann's work and brought to light all of Troy's successive lives —nine in all. According to him Troy VI was Homer's city, destroyed around 1250 BC by Agamemnon's soldiers. An American archaeologist, Carl Blegen—who also dug at the palace in Pylos—challenged this theory during the course of new excavations begun in 1932. He became convinced that Troy VI was destroyed by an earthquake. In his opinion the city sacked by the Greeks of the *Iliad* was Troy VII, or more precisely Troy VIIa (VIIb being merely a resettlement of the ruins of its immediate predecessor).

But this interpretation is shaky. All that can be said with any certainty is that Troy VIIa was destroyed by fire at a date when the Mycenaean world may already have collapsed. The English historian Moses I. Finley has noted that Homer's Trojan War must be lifted out of the history of Bronze Age Greece. That is, according to Finley, the *Iliad* was not the oral transmission of a historical reality. According to recent thinking Homer's epic was a poetic invention that re-created a model past, one that allowed 9th- and 8th-century BC Greek communities to forge their identities "in the shadow of the heroes."

Since 1984 a team from the University of Tübingen in Germany, led by Manfred Korfmann, has been carrying out excavations in Troy. These now make it certain that Ilium—the city which according to ancient tradition was the heir to Troy—did indeed stand on Hissarlik. But the hill was merely the fortified citadel. Ilium itself had

Schliemann's tomb lies in the First Cemetery of Athens, south of the Olympeion and the Ilissos. The archaeologist himself had chosen the site, which boasted a magnificent view. His monument (opposite) was completed in 1892, based on plans drawn up by Ernst Ziller: a small Doric temple on a raised pedestal with a frieze (below) depicting archaeological operations.

occupied a much greater area, proved by the recently
unearthed remains of a defensive wall built one quarter
of a mile south of the area explored by Schliemann.
Troy I, hitherto dated at around 3000 BC, is apparently
less ancient than conjectured, more probably dating from
about 2500 BC. Finally, the site was already occupied
in the fourth millennium before the birth of Christ.
Troy's history was thus much more complex than had
been supposed.

The Hissarlik site as it is today (above). This aerial photo shows the southeastern end of Troy. In the foreground are the fortifications of Troy VI and one of its guard towers. Behind them lie the foundations of a residential building.

### In Praise of the Archaeologist

Schliemann did no more than draw near to the truth.
He was fully aware of this, after striving his whole
life long to close the gap between his dreams and

reality. Eager for wealth and social recognition though he was, his overriding desire was to quench his thirst for knowledge. In his quest for his own and our civilization's origins he was prepared to accept any sacrifice. On the brink of death he was magnanimous enough to accept the refutation of the theories he had defended. Thanks to his determination, he extended the frontiers of Mediterranean archaeology and pushed back the boundaries of time. Before him, Bronze Age Greece was virtually nonexistent. His discovery of Mycenaean civilization gave birth to the study of Aegean protohistory.

Schliemann's excavation techniques have been widely criticized. They caused irreparable damage, but they were, after all, the methods of the day. Nevertheless, he realized that he needed to modernize his methods and eventually acquired the services of a specialist in stratification of the caliber of Wilhelm Dörpfeld. Himself a competent student of pottery, Schliemann was careful not to overlook the smallest on-site clue. His excavation notes were models of conscientiousness; he compiled meticulous excavation reports and carefully labeled the tiniest artifacts. And he was swift to make his findings public. His *Atlas of Trojan Antiquities* was one of the first books to reproduce photographic plates, making it possible for every reader to decide from the evidence on hand. If such practices were faulted, it was because they were ahead of their time.

A fanatical student of historical geography and a tireless traveler, Schliemann was a pioneer prospector. He left two final lessons for his successors: Archaeology is a matter of teamwork—increasingly technical and demanding the participation of experts from diverse scientific disciplines. And, archaeology has to be a profitable activity, constantly dependent on museum connections and oriented toward the general public. Properly conducted, it encourages tourism and fosters the economic interests of the host countries. And such tourism in its turn promotes new vocations for archaeology. After all, it was his own visit to Pompeii that changed the whole course of the life of the businessman from Ankershagen.

"It is now an idle question whether Schliemann, at the beginning of his researches, proceeded from right or wrong presuppositions. Not only has the result decided in his favor, but also the method of his investigation has proved to be excellent....Who would have undertaken such great works, continued through so many years—have spent such large means out of his own fortune—have dug through layers of debris heaped one on the other in a series that seemed almost endless, down to the deep-lying virgin soil—except a man who was penetrated with an assured, nay an enthusiastic conviction? The Burned City would still have lain to this day hidden in the earth, had not imagination guided the spade."

Rudolf Virchow

# DOCUMENTS

"I [Poseidon] walled the city [of Troy]
massively in well-cut stone, to make
the place impregnable"
Homer, *Iliad*
Book XXI, lines 521–23
(trans. Fitzgerald)

# A Who's Who of Homer

*Schliemann was guided through his expeditions by the words of the great poet Homer, who lived in Greece in the 8th century* BC. *The characters of the* Iliad *and the* Odyssey *fueled the archaeologist's imagination as well as his life's work.*

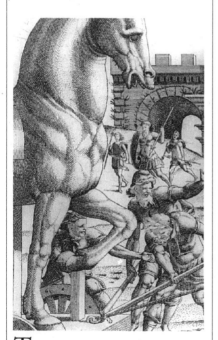

T he Trojan horse in a 19th-century engraving.

### The *Iliad* and the *Odyssey*

*The* Iliad *was probably composed around 750 BC, and it tells of the war between the Trojans and the Greeks. The war began over the abduction of Helen, wife of the Greek king, Menelaus, by the handsome Trojan prince, Paris. Historians today date the Trojan War to about 1250 BC. According to Homer, the Greeks finally succeeded in penetrating the enormous walls of Troy (on the coast of modern-day Turkey) by leaving a huge wooden horse outside the gates, presumably as an offering. When the curious Trojans wheeled the "gift horse" into their citadel, Greek soldiers piled out of it and thus penetrated the city.*

*The* Odyssey, *most probably written some years after the* Iliad, *is the story of Odysseus's ten-year return from the Trojan War back to his native Greece.*

*The main characters in Homer's epics are a fascinating group; their histories are summarized below.*

ACHILLES: Credited with being the Greek's best fighter. In a piratical foray en route to Troy, Achilles's share of the booty is a pretty young woman named Briseis. But Agamemnon, as the expedition's commander in chief, demands her for himself, infuriating Achilles, who broods in his tent while the Trojans defeat the Greeks in battle after battle. He is eventually roused from his tent when his best friend, Patrocles, is killed; spurred to action Achilles avenges Patrocles and helps lead the Greeks to victory.

AENEAS: Actually the hero of a great Roman epic, Virgil's *Aeneid*, Aeneas, a native of Troy, nonetheless features in Homer's *Iliad* as well.

Schliemann claimed that he was inspired as a child to discover Troy by the image in a children's history book of Aeneas fleeing his burning city with his aged father on his back and his young son by the hand [see page 18].

AGAMEMNON: King of Mycenae, brother to the wronged King Menelaus, and the richest and most powerful of the Greek kings, for these reasons chosen to head the expedition to Troy. His greed and pride precipitate a row with Achilles that nearly wrecks the Greek cause. While he is away his wife, Clytemnestra, takes a lover, then has Agamemnon murdered when he returns.

When Schliemann discovered a gold funerary mask at Mycenae, he is said to have exclaimed, "I have gazed upon the face of Agamemnon!"

AJAX. Next to Achilles, the best Greek fighter. Actually Ajax may have lived earlier, but his exploits were so extraordinary that bards gave him a role in the Trojan story.

HECTOR: Priam's son and Troy's finest warrior. Hector leads the besieged Trojans to victory in a series of skirmishes beneath the city's walls. In one of these actions he kills Achilles's closest friend, Patrocles. This forces Achilles to action; he challenges Hector to single combat and, after chasing him around the walls of Troy, kills him. In a touching scene in the *Iliad*, the old and defeated King Priam goes to the enemy camp and begs the Greeks to return the body of his son.

HELEN: Paris's seduction and abduction of the dazzlingly beautiful Helen, wife of King Menelaus, triggers the Trojan War. Despite her infidelity, Homer treats her gently in the *Iliad*, and in the *Odyssey*, she and Menelaus are reconciled.

MENELAUS: King of Sparta and brother to Agamemnon. His wife, Helen, runs off with a young Trojan prince, so Menelaus appeals to Agamemnon for help in seeking revenge. Agamemnon responds by organizing the expedition to Troy.

NESTOR: King of Pylos and probably the second-ranking man on the Greek side. Older than the other commanders, and presumably wiser, he persists in giving long, windy advice to his fellow warriors.

Schliemann hoped to find Nestor's palace in Pylos, but never began excavations.

ODYSSEUS: King of Ithaca, and the most complex and interesting of the *Iliad*'s heroes. A favorite of the later Classical Greeks because—though not the strongest man around—he triumphs by his wits. Homer's *Odyssey* is about Odysseus's ten-year adventure trying to get home after the fall of Troy.

Schliemann thought he had found the Palace of Odysseus in Ithaca.

PARIS: Also Priam's son, a handsome young man who, in his youth, was inveigled into judging which of three goddesses was the most beautiful. He chose Aphrodite, who, as a reward, arranged for Paris's seduction of Helen, the world's most beautiful woman, precipitating the Trojan War.

PRIAM: King of Troy. An old man, unable to fight himself, he senses that his city is doomed, that he and his sons will die, and that his wife Hecuba and all the other Trojan noblewomen will be carried off into slavery.

Schliemann called the gold that he found at Troy the "Treasure of Priam."

Adapted from *The Lost World of the Aegean*
Maitland A. Edey
1975

# Schliemann's Writings

*Schliemann's extensive travel diaries and excavation journals have their own particular flavor—a blend of scientific considerations, calculating personal "confessions," and anecdotes. Here we see what daily life could be like on an excavation site.*

B elow: an 18th-century drawing of Homer reciting his verse. Opposite: Odysseus strapped himself to the mast of his ship so that he would not be tempted by the beautiful music of the deadly sirens.

### The Journey to Ithaca

*In 1869 Schliemann published* Ithaca, the Peloponnese, Troy *in the form of a travel diary. The book conveys the first excitement and enthusiasm of the novice excavator (and earned him a doctorate from the University of Rostock). Here Schliemann seeks the Palace of Odysseus in Ithaca.*

On 10 July, after swimming in the sea and drinking a cup of black coffee, I set out with my workers at five in the morning. At seven, bathed in sweat, we reached the top of Mount Aëtos.

First I had the four men uproot the undergrowth and then start digging at the northeast corner where, I surmised, the famous olive tree once stood—the tree of which Odysseus made his nuptial bed and around which he built his bed chamber [*Odyssey*, Book XXIII, lines 216–27, Fitzgerald trans.];
"An old trunk of olive
grew like a pillar on the building plot,
and I laid out our bedroom round
    that tree,

lined up the stone walls, built the walls
and roof,
gave it a doorway and smooth-fitting
doors.
Then I lopped off the silvery leaves and
branches,
hewed and shaped that stump from the
roots up
into a bedpost, drilled it, let it serve
as model for the rest. I planed them all,
inlaid them all with silver, gold and
ivory,
and stretched a bed between—a pliant web
of oxhide thongs dyed crimson."

But we found nothing beyond
fragments of tile and earthenware, and
two feet down we reached bare rock.
There were admittedly many crevices in
this rock, which the roots of the [olive]
tree could have penetrated; but all hope
of finding archaeological objects there
had disappeared as far as I could tell.

Next I ordered them to dig in the
adjacent earth, for I had found two
rocks there of considerable size, which
seemed once to have formed part of a
wall; and after three hours' work my
men uncovered the two lower layers of
a small building some ten feet wide and
fifteen feet long; the door opening was
three feet in width. The stones were
well cut and measured thirteen inches
square; they were joined together by a
quantity of snow-white cement, pieces
of which I have kept. There was a thick
layer of this cement even beneath the
lower bed of stones. The presence of
this cement convinces me that the
building was erected at least seven
centuries after the Trojan War, for I
have never seen cement in buildings of
the heroic age....

While my laborers were busy with this
excavation, I examined the whole site of
Odysseus's palace with the most careful
attention. Having discovered a large
stone, one of whose ends seemed to
describe a gentle curve—perhaps the

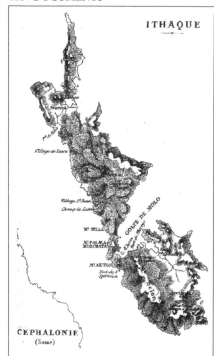

ITHAQUE

CEPHALONIE
(Same)

M ap of Odysseus's kingdom from
Schliemann's *Ithaca, the Peloponnese,
Troy.* Opposite: A view of Ithaca, c. 1820.

hundredth part of a circle—I detached
the earth from the stone with a knife,
and found that the [whole] stone formed
a half-circle. Continuing to probe with
the knife, I swiftly realized that the circle
had been completed on the other side by
small stones set one on the other and
forming a kind of miniature wall. I first
sought to disengage this circle with my
knife, but to no avail: the earth, mingled
with a white substance I recognized as
burned bone-ash, was almost as hard as
stone. I therefore had to dig with a
pickax, but I had barely progressed four
inches before I shattered a fine but very

small vase filled with human ashes. I
then continued to dig with the greatest
care, and uncovered some twenty vases
of curious shape and each one quite
distinct from its fellows. Some lay on
their sides; others were upright. But
unfortunately, due to the hardness of the
earth and my lack of appropriate tools, I
broke most of them as I extracted them,
and was able to recover only five in good
condition. The biggest of them is but
four inches high, with a mouth less than
half an inch across; another had an
opening two inches across. Two of these
vases had quite handsome paintings of
men when I removed them from the
earth. These paintings disappeared
almost as soon as I exposed them to the
sun, but I hope to revive them by
rubbing them with alcohol and water.

All these vases were filled with the
ashes of burned human bodies.

In this small domestic graveyard I
also found the curved blade of a
sacrificial knife, five inches long, and
rust-covered, but otherwise well
preserved; a terracotta idol depicting a
goddess with two flutes at her lips; then
the remains of an iron sword, a boar's
tooth, several small animal bones, and
finally a handle made of woven bronze
wires. I would have given five years of
my life for an inscription—but alas,
there was none!

Although the age of these artifacts is
difficult to determine, it seems certain
to me that the vases are much older
than those from Cumae at the Naples
Museum, and it is quite possible that in
my five little urns I hold the bodies of
Ulysses and Penelope or of their
offspring!

Having excavated the circular pit to
its depths, I measured it: on the south
side it was thirty inches deep, and on

the north thirty-six inches, while its diameter was four feet.

There is nothing more thirst-provoking than the rough job of digging in 120 degrees in the sun. We had brought with us three huge water-jugs and a large bottle containing four liters of wine. The wine was quite enough [for our needs], since the product of Ithaca grapes is, as I have already said, three times stronger than Bordeaux wine; but our supply of water was soon exhausted, and we were twice obliged to replenish it.

My four workmen completed their excavation of the post-Homeric dwelling just as I finished unearthing the little circular grave-pit. I had been more successful than they; but I bore them no ill-will, for they had worked hard, and another thousand years may go by before the site is once again blanketed with dust.

[By now] It was noon, and we had eaten nothing since five that morning; we therefore sat down to lunch beneath an olive tree between the two enclosing walls, some fifty feet below the summit. Our meal consisted of dry bread, wine and water whose temperature was around eighty-seven degrees Fahrenheit. But I was eating the fruit of the soil of Ithaca, and eating it in the courtyard of Odysseus's palace, and perhaps on the very spot where that king wept as his favorite dog Argos died of joy on recognizing his master again after twenty years' absence.

Heinrich Schliemann
*Ithaca, the Peloponnese, Troy*, 1869

# In Search of Love

*After his first disastrous marriage, Heinrich Schliemann was determined to find himself a more compatible mate. In his novel about the archaeologist, writer Irving Stone describes Schliemann's "interview" (based on Schliemann's own accounts) with a prospective bride, thirty years his junior.*

Heinrich and Sophia Schliemann, c. 1880.

Henry Schliemann hired the largest sailboat available but it seemed pitifully small and frail to Sophia [who was afraid of the sea]. The trip out of the harbor was calm, and she had hopes of coming through the afternoon without disgracing herself. But the moment the boat left the protected bay and entered the open sea the sun vanished behind a cloud, a wind sprang up and the sailboat began to pitch to and fro. Sophia became queasy....

"Miss Sophia," he began in an earnest, affectionate tone, "why do you want to marry me?"

"Oh no," thought Sophia, "not at this moment! When I am about to lean over the railing."

There was no escaping his intense gaze, or the tense posture of his head on his neck as he awaited the all-important answer to his question.... She answered as honestly as she could:

"Because my parents have told me to."

She saw Henry Schliemann turn pale. For an instant she thought he was the one to be sick. Then anger thundered into his eyes; she had never seen them blazing this way before. Outraged color flooded upward on the lean cheeks. His voice was hoarse.

"I am deeply pained, Miss Sophia, at the answer you have given me, one worthy of a slave; and all the more strange because it comes from an educated young woman. I myself am a simple, honorable, home-loving man. If ever we were married, it would be so that we could excavate together and share our common love of Homer."

The seas had grown rougher. The sailboat was surrounded by white-caps. ... Nauseous as she was, she had better set this strange and unpredictable man straight.

"Mr. Henry, you should not be shocked by my answer. The marriage of every girl in Greece is arranged by her parents, who conscientiously try to find her the best possible husband. That is what my parents have done and I accept their judgment. It is a quality you should value in me: if I am a good daughter, it means I will be a good wife."

Only partly appeased, Henry demanded in a quieter but still stern voice:

"Is there no other reason why you are willing to marry me? Surely there must be something in your decision besides blind obedience?"

…Making a desperate effort to formulate her thoughts, she murmured to herself:

"But what other answer is he looking for? I have already said that I admire and respect him for the strength of his convictions about Homer. I have already indicated that I have faith in his writings. For what other quality does he want me to admire him, when he has told us that these pursuits are his whole life? That he wants a Greek wife to help him to fulfill his dreams. I have missed something. And how can I think when all I want to do is die?"

Then…she said to herself:

"But of course! The quality for which all the world admires him, and because of which every family in Greece with a daughter to marry has been pursuing him. He is a millionaire! With more money than anyone we've ever heard of! And he achieved it all by himself, without formal education, without family or backing. He has a right to be proud of himself."

She looked up at Henry Schliemann once again, putting all the admiration and pride into her voice that she could muster, paying him the world's ultimate compliment:

"Because you are rich!"

Henry's face became stony.

"You want to marry me, not for my value as a human being, but because I am rich! I am no longer in a position to converse with you. I have decided not to think of you any more."

He turned away, calling curtly to the crew:

"Put back into port."

Irving Stone
*The Greek Treasure*, 1975

### An Anniversary Letter

*Despite their rather rocky start, Heinrich and Sophia were eventually married. On the eve of their twenty-first wedding anniversary, Heinrich wrote his wife a letter.*

…Today, as I look back at the long time I have spent with you, I see that the Fates have spun us many sorrows and many joys. We are accustomed to look at the past through rose-colored spectacles, forgetting the past woes and remembering only the pleasant things. I cannot praise our marriage enough. You have never ceased being a loving wife to me, a good comrade, and an unfailing guide in difficulties, as well as a loving companion and a mother like no other. I am so delighted with the virtues with which I see you adorned that I have already agreed to marry you in the coming life.

Letter to Sophia Schliemann from
Heinrich Schliemann
23 September 1890
Excerpted in David Traill
*Schliemann of Troy*
1995

# Mycenae

*At Mycenae, relations between the Schliemanns and Panagiotis Stamatakis, the official representative of the Greek Archaeological Society, were far from smooth. Not over-endowed with tact, the couple behaved unfairly to one of the most gifted Greek archaeologists of his generation. Here is the Greek scientist's version of events as he reported them to his superiors.*

Drawing of the Lion Gate, Mycenae, 1877. Opposite: Sophia Schliemann surveys the Mycenaean excavations.

The morning of Thursday 24 August, when I arrived at the site I saw that excavation had begun on the underground chamber. I had told Mr. Schliemann that I could not supervise this new enterprise and consequently could not authorize it. He replied in a hostile manner, as is his custom, that he was going to clean out the entrance to the underground chamber and that if I was not equal to the task, Ministry would send more officials. I replied that the Ministry had granted permission for an excavation with fifty to sixty workmen, not with ninety workmen, and not with workmen paid by the cubic meter. He answered that he had permission to have as many excavations as he wished and under whatever terms he wished and that my only task was to receive the finds. I pointed out that my mission was not merely to receive the finds but also to have general supervision over all the work at Mycenae and to prevent any contravention of the law or of the Ministry's instructions. I added that since he had such an opinion of my mission, he should communicate this to the General Ephoria of Antiquities and if it approved the work undertaken, then that was fine. Otherwise, the sites being excavated would be reduced to one so that the collection of the finds could proceed in a proper manner and the workmen could be carefully supervised to prevent them from stealing objects, as it was rumored a few days ago in Argos they were doing, and so that the finds could be properly recorded every day.

The following day at the excavations outside the underground chamber there appeared a line of walling of squared bricks and beside this another wall at a greater depth. In my absence, Schliemann instructed the workmen

to destroy both these walls. When I got there later and learned this, I told the workmen not to destroy the walls before they had been carefully examined and if they appeared insignificant, then they would be destroyed, but if they were important, they should be preserved. While Mr. Schliemann was absent, the workmen followed my instructions. The next day, however, Saturday, Mr. Schliemann came to the site very early, bringing his wife along with him. He instructed the workmen to destroy the walls they had struck against. In case I should try, when I arrived later, to prevent further destruction, he left his wife in charge of the workmen as guardian of his instructions, while he proceeded to the acropolis. When I arrived a little later, I asked the workmen why they were destroying the walls when they were prohibited from doing so. Schliemann's wife answered that I had no right to give such instructions, that her husband was a scholar, that the walls were Roman and that it was appropriate to destroy them because they were impeding the workmen, that I had no idea about such matters, and that I ought not to trouble Mr. Schliemann with such instructions because he was easily provoked and might break off the excavations. I replied that Mr. Schliemann was not entirely free to do as he wished with the ancient objects, as he had done at Troy, and that he had been given a permit to conduct excavations at Mycenae in conformance with the law. Mr. Schliemann, from the very beginning of the excavations, has shown a tendency to destroy, against my wishes, everything Greek or Roman in order that only what he identifies as Pelasgian [prehistoric] houses and tombs remain and be preserved. Whenever potsherds of the Greek and Roman period are uncovered, he treats them with disgust. If in the course of the work they fall into his hands, he throws them away. We, however, collect everything—what he calls Pelasgian, and Greek and Roman pieces.

Panagiotis Stamatakis
Report to General Ephoria of
Antiquities, Athens
Excerpted in David Traill,
*Schliemann of Troy,* 1995

# What Happened to "Priam's Gold"?

*After promising them at various times to Greece, Russia, the United States, England, and France, Schliemann finally bequeathed his Trojan treasures to his native Germany. They were to be exhibited in the Berlin Museums in a special gallery bearing Schliemann's name. The treasures were on exhibit for several decades but were put away for safekeeping during World War II. By the end of the war, however, all the gold had disappeared.*

### A Discovery in the Basement

*The fate of "Priam's Gold" was one of the great mysteries of the war.*

One day in September 1987, Grigorii Kozlov, who had recently become the curator of the new Museum of Private Collections in Moscow, a branch of the Pushkin Museum, was asked by a colleague to make photocopies of some papers. In 1987 this was still a formidable task. Copying machines were rare in the Soviet Union, and there were none in the Pushkin Museum. But Kozlov had worked in the Ministry of Culture and had friends there, and he thought he could use his connections to get access to a copier.

…When Kozlov reached the fourth floor, where the Department of Visual Arts was located, he saw piles of papers and books strewn about in complete disorder. At first he thought there had been an accident of some sort. Then he saw a former colleague, G., walking toward him with a heap of old documents under his arms.

"What's going on?" Kozlov asked him?… Kozlov's friend told him that the chief of the Department of Museums had decided to clean out old papers and other "junk." They had already thrown away tons of documents, he said, and then he asked Kozlov to help him carry a batch to the basement, where they would be destroyed. Kozlov took part of the load and followed him.… Finally they stopped, and G. knocked on a door that was opened by a woman wearing dirty white overalls and a gauze mask and rubber gloves. She was carrying a long knife.

"Ach, they've brought more," she said to someone inside. The room was dimly lit by a couple of unshaded lightbulbs hanging from the ceiling, and the air was full of dust. Another woman, similarly attired, was standing at a big metal table heaped with bundles of old documents, cutting the strings and throwing the papers into a pile on the floor. At the other end of the room there was a shredding machine. The woman who had opened the door showed the men where to put their loads. In the dim light Kozlov noticed that a sheet of paper lying on the floor near his foot had the words "State Pushkin Museum" at the top. He picked it up and began to read. G. was in a hurry and left Kozlov alone with the two women.

"May I see the papers?" Kozlov asked them....

"Sure," answered the older one. "Take a knife and cut the strings. Your help is welcome."

Kozlov was having trouble breathing in the dusty air, and he made a mask of his handkerchief. As he opened the bundles, he glanced quickly over each paper. On the sheet he had picked up from the floor, he had noticed something that made his heart skip a beat. Near the name of the museum was written in red pencil the word "restitution." The word conjured up an event that he had until recently thought he knew all about: the Soviet Union's return to East Germany in 1955 of the masterpieces taken from the Dresden Gallery at the end of World War II. The "rescue" of the Dresden Gallery had been the major cultural event of the war as far as the Soviet Union was concerned, and its restitution ten years later was a milestone in the relations between the two countries....

Could there be artworks removed from Germany that were still hidden in storerooms in the Soviet Union—great and famous masterpieces that the world believed destroyed or lost?

Now cutting the strings and sorting quickly through the brittle papers in the cellar of the Ministry of Culture, Kozlov hoped to find answers to some of his questions. He could see that the documents were important. After half an hour of digging in the dusty heaps, he found what he wanted: minutes of the Soviet-German negotiations for the return of the Dresden Gallery pictures and papers dealing with their exhibition in Moscow before they were sent back to Germany. Koslov kept on sorting through the papers, hoping for more information. Then he turned up something that made him gasp: a handwritten document entitled "List of the Most Important Art Works Kept in the Special Depository of the Pushkin Museum." Another document, entitled "Unique Objects from the 'Large Trojan Treasure,' Berlin, Museum für Völkerkunde," was signed by Nora Ellasberg, acting chief curator of the Pushkin Museum, and dated March 28, 1957. Kozlov had in his hands evidence that the famous Trojan treasure excavated by Heinrich Schliemann in 1873, which had mysteriously disappeared from Berlin in 1945, had not been destroyed but had been hidden in the Soviet Union for more than forty years.

The "Trojan Treasure" listed in Nora Eliasberg's inventory was more than simply one of the greatest archaeological discoveries in history. From the moment Heinrich Schliemann announced to the world that he had found the treasure of King Priam of Troy, the ancient gold and silver objects had exerted a special hold over the popular imagination. Had Priam himself poured wine into this small gold goblet? Had Helen of Troy worn these diadems and adorned her fingers with the gold rings?

Schliemann was a rich German businessman and amateur archaeologist obsessed with proving that the Trojan War had been a real event, not just a legend handed down by generations of bards to the blind Homer. He believed that Priam and Helen, Hector and Agamemnon were real people. The discovery of the golden hoard was his proof....

In 1881 Schliemann presented the treasure to the German nation, "in perpetual possession and inalienable custody," and museum officials promised that it would be on view in Berlin for all time. It remained there for sixty years, first in the Ethnographic Museum and then in the Museum for Pre- and Early History.

In 1939, as war became imminent, officials of the Berlin State Museums were told to safeguard their precious possessions, and all the exhibits of the Museum for Pre- and Early History were packed up and trundled down to the basement. Objects made of precious metals and those that were considered irreplaceable, including most of the objects from Troy, were packed into three crates. An inventory list was stuck into each crate, and they were sealed. In January 1941 most of the museum's exhibits, including the three crates, were moved to the vault of the Prussian State Bank to protect them from air bombardment. Later that year they were moved again, to one of the new fortresslike antiaircraft towers that Albert Speer's workshop had designed to protect the capital of the Reich. Two of these steel-and-concrete behemoths, which were considered impregnable, were earmarked as repositories for Berlin's cultural treasures. The Museum for Pre- and Early History was assigned two rooms on the north side of the tower near the Zoological Garden—the Zoo Flakturm.

The Zoo tower, occupying almost an entire city block, was the largest of the Flakturm. From its roof, the Luftwaffe directed the defense of Berlin, firing off 128-mm guns with a deafening boom. Ammunition was stored deep below ground and brought up in steel elevators. The museum's exhibits remained in the tower until 1945, by which time the surrounding area had been reduced to rubble. The zoo had been destroyed and most of the animals killed. A team of veterinarians chopped up the carcasses of the dead elephants to be processed into soap and

A bust of Sophia Schliemann wearing the headpiece from the "Treasure of Priam."

bonemeal, and hungry Berliners were said to be cooking crocodile tails and sausage made of dead bears.

In February 1945 the directors of the Prussian State Museums were ordered to evacuate all their collections to an area west of the Elbe River that had been designated as an American and British occupation zone if there were to be a surrender. The Germans didn't want their treasures to fall into Russian hands. But the museum directors thought it would be so dangerous to move the collections on highways, railways, or waterways subject to enemy bombing that they were unwilling to obey the order. Hitler himself was consulted, and in March a "Führer's Order" was issued. The art was moved.

Marshal Georgy Zhukov, deputy supreme commander of the Red Army and leader of the assault on Berlin, launched the final battle for the capital on April 16, 1945. By this time, most of the art treasures had left the city, headed for several salt mines. Many ended up in Merkers, where they were found by General Patton's Third Army. Several thousand crates filled with artworks and archaeological objects, including fifty from the Museum for Pre- and Early History, were discovered in Grasleben by the U.S. First Army. But the three crates containing the Trojan gold had a different fate.

Dr. Wilhelm Unverzagt, director of the Museum for Pre- and Early History and a loyal Nazi, had obeyed Hitler's order to transport his collection out of the city—except for the three precious crates. He didn't want them to leave Berlin, and as the Red Army attacked the Zoo tower he remained with the crates, sleeping on top of them at night. The din of battle was made more horrible by the groans of the wounded from the hospital that had been set up in a nearby room. Corpses and amputated limbs piled up. Terrified civilians who had fled the bombardment were crammed in so tightly that they could hardly move. The city was in flames.

The devoted Unverzagt remained in the tower after everyone else had fled. On the first of May, the day after Hitler's suicide, it was surrendered to the Russians. They swarmed in, clattering up and down the staircases looking for loot. Unverzagt stood his ground until a senior officer appeared. He told him about the treasure packed in the crates and asked for his help. The officer posted guards at the door of the room. A few days later, Colonel General Nikolai Berzarin, the Soviet commander of the city, came to inspect the tower and assured Unverzagt that the crates would be taken to a safe place. At the end of May, the three crates containing the Trojan gold were loaded onto a Studebaker truck. Unverzagt never saw them again.

The fate of Priam's gold was one of the great mysteries of the Second World War. Scholars had been attempting to track it down for over four decades by the time Grigorii Kozlov picked up the piece of paper on the basement floor that indicated that the treasure was locked away somewhere in Moscow's Pushkin Museum, a refugee from yet another siege and the sacking of a great city.

Konstantin Akinsha and
Grigorii Kozlov
*Beautiful Loot:
The Soviet Plunder of
Europe's Art Treasures*
1995

# "Priam's Gold" on Display

*For almost fifty years the golden artifacts that Schliemann gave to the city of Berlin were thought to have been lost, stolen, or even melted down. In fact, however, they were taken, along with other treasures, by Soviet troops in the last days of the war and brought to Russia. In 1994 the Pushkin Museum announced that it was holding the "Treasure of Priam" among its collections. German officials came to Moscow and inspected the golden objects at the museum, where the "Treasure of Priam" will be exhibited for the first time since the war. Its future is unknown.*

### Treasures at the Pushkin

*Vladimir Tolstikov is head of the Department of Art and Archaeology of the Ancient World at the Pushkin State Museum for Fine Arts in Moscow. Mikhail Treister is senior researcher and curator of the same department.*

The collection of Trojan antiquities that is now at the Pushkin Museum has a complicated and dramatic history. From the very beginning some of the objects were removed from Troy by Heinrich Schliemann illegally, without the permission of Turkish authorities. Later the collection was given by Schliemann as a gift to the German nation and housed in Berlin. At the start of the Second World War the most valuable pieces of the Berlin collection (thirteen of the original nineteen hoards, known as Treasures A to S) were packed in boxes and hidden away. Only recently has the public learned that in 1945 these crates were collected by Soviet troops and shipped to Moscow. Most of the bronze vessels and axes that were part of the Berlin collection are now in the Hermitage Museum in Saint Petersburg; while other pieces, such as the group known as Treasure C (which were in fact stolen by Schliemann's workers), found their way to the Archaeological Museum in Istanbul after the thieves were apprehended. And still another group, mainly beads, was given by Sophia Schliemann after her husband's death to the National Archaeological Museum of Athens.

Only a few scholars have been allowed to examine the objects at the Pushkin Museum since their resurfacing, among them the prominent Bronze Age scholar Machteld Mellink from Bryn

Mawr, Donald Easton, an English expert on Schliemann, and Manfred Korfmann from Germany, head of the "Troy Project," who has been leading excavations at Troy since the late 1980s. However, the very first to examine the pieces as they emerged from storage were representatives of Berlin's Museum for Pre- and Early History, who visited the Pushkin in October 1994. The Berlin team was astonished at the excellent preservation and storage of the objects, all of which still have their German accession numbers. The original packing material was not kept, but the objects had been carefully weighed, packed into new crates, and hidden away for almost fifty years. In the late 1940s some Soviet archaeologists were fortunate enough to catch a glimpse of the treasures, but the new generation of Russian scholars had no idea of the whereabouts of the world-famous archaeological finds. Although there were often rumors....

Treasure A, also known as Priam's Treasure, includes gold and silver vessels (among them the famous "sauceboat"), earrings, bracelets, and beads. But the finest pieces are two gold diadems composed of chain links and thousands of tiny golden leaves. The larger diadem was immortalized in the famous photograph of Sophia Schliemann [see page 44].

American philologist David Traill once suggested that "Priam's Treasure" might be a fraudulent collection of items, amassed from different sites. Our evidence, however, points to the authenticity of the pieces. Important to this argument is the composition of the treasures, which matches what we know about the economic situation of pre-historic Troy—the wealth of its people and the materials available to its artisans—and makes improbable the forgery theory.

The most plausible date for the objects is around the middle third quarter of the third millennium BC, which corresponds well to the date of the burned level of Troy IIg. (Manfred Korfmann dates this to c. 2600–2450 BC based on stratigraphy of the settlement and carbon dating.) By around 2500 BC Troy, located at the crossroads of maritime and overland trade routes between Europe and Asia, had become a center of prosperity, attracting the finest artisans of the ancient world.

We are still uncertain of the specific functions of the various pieces; they may have belonged to temples, rulers, goldsmiths, or served several different roles in Trojan society.

What will happen with the collection after the Moscow exhibition? The question of whether it will stay in Moscow or be returned to Germany has not yet been resolved, although a joint Russian-German commission on restitution has been meeting since 1993. Meanwhile the Russian parliament has issued a moratorium on the return of cultural treasures, which is understandable, given the numerous losses of Russian monuments and art works during the war.

Although the future of the Trojan Treasures is not known, it is clear that the objects are of tremendous cultural and scientific importance to the world and must be made accessible to the international community of scholars as well as the general public.

Vladimir Tolstikov and
Mikhail Treister
1996

# Distinguishing Fact from Fiction

*In his lifetime Heinrich Schliemann was called a liar, a forger, and a cheat; while few today dispute his enormous contributions to archaeology and our knowledge of ancient Greece, the abuse continues to fly. Has criticism of Schliemann been carried too far?*

Terracotta idol from Mycenae.

### A Case for the Prosecution

*David Traill has scrupulously analyzed Schliemann's diaries, letters, and publications, finding in them a litany of discrepancies.*

It is of course his lying and penchant for fraud that are of greatest importance when we consider Schliemann's career as an archaeologist. The prevalence of lies in Schliemann's writings and the peculiar quality of many of them suggest that his lying was pathological. Consider for instance, his "eyewitness" account of the fire of San Francisco or his interview with President Fillmore, both in his 1851–2 diary. There is also the bizarre entry in the 1869 diary, in which he insists that he will have nothing to do with the "horrors" of "false certificates and perjury" to obtain a New York divorce on the very day on which he obtained his American citizenship by these means. Here too Schliemann's behavior improved as he grew older. The influence of Virchow from 1879 onwards and Schliemann's efforts to please and emulate him were no doubt factors in this improvement.

Schliemann almost certainly fabricated the story concerning his original impetus toward archaeology. The evidence points overwhelmingly to the conclusion that Schliemann had no childhood dream of excavating Troy. What was it then that prompted him to devote the last twenty years of his life to Homeric archaeology? The answer may surprise and disappoint, but it is quite clear. He fell into it. In the spring of 1868 he planned to return to St. Petersburg to see his children. His route was to take him via Italy, Greece, and the Black Sea. Ithaca and

Troy were to be stops on the way, since he had missed them on his previous Grand Tour. Discussions at the learned societies in Paris had stimulated his interest in Homeric sites but the thought of actually excavating them seems not to have even occurred to him at this stage. The news that he would face renewed litigation in St Petersburg forced him to abandon his visit to Russia. This allowed him to take a much more leisurely trip than he had originally planned....

How then are we to assess Schliemann's excavations? The greatness of his achievements and their enduring significance are beyond dispute. But given his propensities, the question naturally arises, how much can we believe? His archaeological reports clearly provide, *for the most part,* a reliable record of his excavations. That is not in dispute. On the other hand, the comforting formula that he told lies in his private life but not in his archaeology is no longer tenable. Neither can we say that he told lies in his published work but not in his diaries. There are a great many lies in the diaries. We need to be skeptical at all times, but especially when it comes to the most dramatic finds.

Consider Priam's Treasure. Sophia did not witness the discovery in May 1873 as Schliemann reports. She was in Athens at the time. Schliemann's earliest account placed the findspot in a room in the so-called Priam's Palace. Later the findspot was moved to the city wall "directly next to Priam's Palace." But all the plans place it just *outside* the city wall. This coincides with the testimony of Yannakis [Schliemann's foreman at Troy]. The earliest accounts imply a discovery

date of 31 May. Later this was changed to 7 June. Several pieces that appear in photographs of Priam's Treasure also appear in photographs taken in 1872 of the previous two years' finds. The gold jewelry is not mentioned in the earliest accounts of the discovery. Should we accept Schliemann's account as essentially true with a few honest mistakes, or was Priam's Treasure actually a more modest find of bronze and silver pieces enhanced by the season's unreported gold pieces and even some earlier finds? The building just within the Scaean Gate, which he identified as Priam's Palace, was not very impressive. Was the treasure a dramatic attempt to authenticate it?

In 1882 very few of the season's more valuable finds ever reached the museum in Constantinople. It is clear from Schliemann's correspondence with Virchow that he was carefully keeping his best finds hidden from the Turks. Accordingly, when he came to write up his report, he could assign his finds to whatever part he wanted. He reported that the overwhelmingly bulk of the more interesting pieces came from what was now the most impressive building in Troy II: "Temple (later Megaron) A." This looks like another instance of Schliemann "bundling" his best finds in much the same way he seems to have done in 1873 and for similar reasons.

In his later excavations, Schliemann resorted less frequently to dishonesty. It is hard to imagine, for instance, that there are many serious distortions in his reports on Orchomenos and Tiryns. On the other hand, in 1890 he smuggled all the best finds—the stone axes, the silver vase, and the marble heads—past the Turkish supervisors and off to Athens. He thereby deceived Hamdy Bey [Director of the Imperial Museum in Constantinople], who courteously allowed him to take the pottery, which legally belonged to the Turkish government. Even at the end of his life he could act in an unprincipled manner towards those who helped him and he had no qualms about paying the workmen who brought him finds clandestinely. His success and the ineffectiveness of the supervision are all the more remarkable in that the Turks knew from 1873 onwards that Schliemann was a wily and unscrupulous manipulator, who needed to be watched very carefully.

What then of Mycenae? The extraordinary wealth of Shaft Graves III, IV, and V has never been adequately explained. A noted expert on the finds comments on the "startling discrepancies in quality and organization of design." May not the great wealth and "startling discrepancies" of these tombs be attributable to more "bundling" by Schliemann? It is clear that Schliemann came across quite a few tombs and burials long before he reached the shaft graves. There were rich finds of bronzes in some of these tombs. There may well have also been gold pieces, smuggled past Stamatakis [the Greek archaeologist appointed to watch over Schliemann at Mycenae] to Schliemann by the workmen for payment and then saved for the grand finale: Shaft Graves III, IV, and V. At Troy in 1882 Schliemann paid local villagers to make clandestine excavations in the surrounding area. In 1876 he was well aware that there were rich tholos and chamber tombs in the vicinity of Mycenae. Some of the pieces that seem too late for the shaft graves, like Nestor's Cup, may come from clandestine excavations commissioned by Schliemann. A simple microscopic examination should be able to determine whether there are any modern forgeries among the pieces that occur in multiple copies or, like some of the gold masks, are suspicious for other reasons. If, however, Schliemann added to Shaft Graves III, IV, or V authentic objects that had in fact been found elsewhere it is hard to see how this can now be proved conclusively. Stylistically, a number of pieces seem too late for these graves. Should we trust Schliemann's account of them because it cannot be disproved? Or should we be skeptical because it is hard to reconcile their attribution to these graves with evidence from other excavations?

Archaeologists, historians, and excavators gathered along the Cyclopean walls of Tiryns.

Schliemann was an extraordinary individual. In his life and character there is much to admire and much to deplore. It is hard, and probably misguided, to develop a consistent attitude towards him. His egotism, mendacity, and often cynical behavior inevitably alienate our sympathy. In light of his difficult childhood, however, his flaws become more understandable and one can only admire the unquenchable resolution to improve himself by sheer hard work. A picture emerges of a profoundly contradictory and elusive personality. He strove to become a hero. Although questions remain, and indeed are becoming more insistent, Heinrich Schliemann, thanks to his astonishing success, is likely to remain the emblematic archaeologist of all time.

David Traill
*Schliemann of Troy:*
*Treasure and Deceit*
1995

## In Defense of Schliemann

*Nigel Spivey reviews David Traill's book on Schliemann, finding the biography too harsh a study of the man.*

Traill…has been pursuing the traces of Heinrich Schliemann like a blood-hound for over a decade. Articles accusing Schliemann of diverse crimes have appeared in specialist journals, and were collected in a volume from Illinois called *Excavating Schliemann* in 1993. The present book is a piece of interim vulgarization of the case so far. Cruelly, it is issued by Schliemann's own British publishers, John Murray. Cruel, because David Traill's broad aim—

though of course he murmurs otherwise—is to discredit Schliemann's life and work.

He does this chiefly by insinuation. Traill's fraud-squad investigation into Schliemann is virtually a one-man project, but its launch in 1972 was by the Classical historiographer William Calder III, who programmed a method of attack: demonstrate that Schliemann was duplicitous in his personal and his business life; then infer a "patho-logical mendacity" carried over to Schliemann's archaeological career. Accordingly, much of Traill's chase has been devoted to inaccuracies and falsehoods in Schliemann's diaries, starting with Schliemann's colorful account of the San Francisco fire in 1851—an event at which he is unlikely to have been present, and seems to have written up vicariously from newspaper reports—and then sniffing out evidence of business malpractice, a shifty divorce, and some Walter Mitty-style inventions of meetings with American presidents and such like. So the argument advances: if Schliemann short-changed customers in the days when he was trading gold-dust and indigo, if he lied to his friends, his wives, and himself, then why should we believe his reports of finds at Troy and Mycenae and elsewhere?

Like so many investigations of fraud, however, Traill's enterprise gets so far and then fizzles out. Schliemann was certainly a dodger, and Traill establishes in a manner which is probably definitive the extent to which Schliemann romanticized the first half of his life. The son of a drunken and disgraced Lutheran pastor, Schliemann ostensibly redeemed family honor on two scores. First, he made himself more than respectably rich; second, he achieved academic distinction. Whether he was originally fired to gain that distinction as a boy by seeing pictures of Troy ablaze is, as Traill establishes, highly doubtful. And whether he got rich as a means to the end of academic honor is also unclear. Plainly he adored the sort of trite lionization that academics can muster when they try—the honorary degrees, the medals and so on—and plainly he felt desperately insecure in the world of scholarship, never apparently understanding that since the time of Galileo, scholarly dissension has been permissible. And sometimes he crassly muddled the two worlds of business and academia, as when he offered cash to journal editors for the publication of his articles. But on the whole, Schliemann achieved his double redemption. That he sedulously scripted an already adventurous life into a resounding epic we can surely forgive. His diligence earned at least the right to be pompous.

Beyond this, Traill is hard pushed to make anything stick. That Schliemann compressed, juggled, and generally dramatized his excavation reports can be proven to a point. But insinuations of actual forgery are no more than that. "Priam's Treasure" can be shown to be assembled from different stages of excavation, but it is not forensically demonstrated that Schliemann commissioned fake jewelry to bolster its appeal. Likewise, all that Traill can do with his suspicion that some of the finds from the shaft graves of Mycenae may be forged is tell us that the authorities at the Athens National Museum have so far refused to test the authenticity of the gold mask and other celebrated objects. This falls a long way short of a serious allegation. From the kangaroo court erected by Traill's court, Schliemann ultimately walks away free.

The book is engaging nonetheless. And if nothing else, it prompts some tangential reflections on the rhapsodic capacities of other archaeologists whose careers owe much, indirectly, to the extraordinary public interest raised by Schliemann's pursuit of Homer's heroic world. Do we imagine that Schliemann belongs to a crude age of folly, in his naive efforts to weave marvelous stories about disinterred objects? Then we deceive ourselves. In 1966, Carl Blegen entitled his excavations at Mycenae Pylos: "The Palace of Nestor." In 1988, Italian archaeologists on the Palatine Hill in Rome spoke of finding "The Wall of Romulus." It was early this year that the world was rashly telegraphed that the tomb of Alexander had been located in the Egyptian oasis of Siwa. And it was only a year or two ago that the first plaintive sagas began to be woven, by the sort of archaeologists who wear white coats, of the life and times of the "Ice Man" lately recovered from the Austro-Italian borders. These are random instances of a force which bears upon all composers of history: the breeze of inspiration from Clio, a muse. She wants more than a catalogue of relics. She demands stories, heroes, spilt blood, and enchantments. We should consider Schliemann's faults in this perspective: a case of Clio's derangement, nothing more, and nothing less.

Nigel Spivey
*Times Literary Supplement*
1995

# Further Reading

WORKS BY SCHLIEMANN
Schliemann wrote in several languages. The following works by him are noted in their original edition:

La Chine et le Japon au Temps Présent, Librairie Centrale, Paris, 1867

Ithaque, le Péloponnèse, Troie. Recherches Archéologiques, Reinwald, Paris, 1869

Trojanische Alterhümer. Bericht über die Ausgrabungen in Troja (with atlas), F.A. Brockhaus, Leipzig, 1874

Mycenae: a Narrative of Researches and Discoveries at Mycenae and Tiryns, John Murray, London, 1878

Ilios: the City and Country of the Trojans, John Murray, London, 1880

Orchomenos: Bericht über meine Ausgrabungen, F.A. Brockhaus, Leipzig, 1881

Tiryns: the Prehistoric Palace of the Kings of Tiryns, Scribner's Sons, New York, 1885; John Murray, London, 1886

Troja: Results of the Latest Researches and Discoveries on the Site of Homer's Troy, John Murray, London, and Harper & Bros., New York, 1884

Troy and Its Remains, John Murray, London, 1875

THE CORRESPONDENCE OF SCHLIEMANN
Hermann, J., and Evelin Maaß, Die Korrespondenz zwischen Heinrich Schliemann und Rudolf Virchow, Akademie Verlag, Berlin, 1990

Meyer, Ernst, ed., Briefe von Heinrich Schliemann, Walter de Gruyter, Berlin, 1936

ON THE LIFE OF SCHLIEMANN
Calder, William M., III, "Schliemann on Schliemann: A Study in the Use of Sources," Greek, Roman, and Byzantine Studies 13, pp. 335–53, 1972

——— and Justus Cobet, Heinrich Schliemann nach Hundert Jahren (text of a lecture delivered at the symposium marking the 100th anniversary of the death of Schliemann), Klostermann, Frankfurt am Main, 1990

——— and David Traill, Myth, Scandal, and History: The Heinrich Schliemann Controversy and a First Edition of the Mycenaean Diary, Wayne State University, Detroit, 1986

Deuel, Leo, Memoirs of Heinrich Schliemann, Harper & Row, New York and London, 1977

Lehrer, Mark, and David Turner, "The Making of an Archaeologist: Schliemann's Diary of 1868," Annual of the British School at Athens 84, pp. 221–68, 1989

Lilly, Eli, ed., Schliemann in Indianapolis, Indiana

Historical Society, Indianapolis, 1961

Ludwig, Emil. Schliemann: The Story of a Gold-Seeker, Little Brown, Boston, 1931

Moorehead, Caroline, The Lost Treasures of Troy, Weidenfeld & Nicolson, London, 1994

Payne, Robert, The Gold of Troy: The Story of Heinrich Schliemann and the Buried Cities of Ancient Greece, Robert Hale, London, 1959

Poole, Lynn and Gray, One Passion, Two Loves: The Story of Heinrich and Sophia Schliemann, Discoverers of Troy, Crowell, New York, 1966

Schuchhardt, Carl, Schliemann's Excavations: An Archaeological and Historical Study, Macmillan, London, 1891

Stone, Irving, The Greek Treasure, Doubleday, New York, 1975

Traill, David, Schliemann of Troy, John Murray, London, 1995

Turner, David, "Heinrich Schliemann: The Man Behind the Masks," Archaeology, Nov/Dec, pp. 36–42, 1990

Weber, Shirley H., ed., Schliemann's First Visit to America, 1850–51, Gennadius Monographs, no. 2, Harvard University Press for the American

School of Classical Studies at Athens, Cambridge, Mass., 1942

OTHER WORKS
Blegen, Carl, Troy: Excavations Conducted by the University of Cincinnati, 1932–8, 4 vols., Princeton University Press, 1950–8

———, Troy and the Trojans, Thames and Hudson, London, and Praeger, New York, 1963

Cook, J.M., The Troad: An Archaeological and Topographical Study, Oxford University Press, 1973

Cottrell, Leonard, Realms of Gold: A Journey in Search of the Mycenaeans, New York Graphic Society, 1963

Edey, Maitland, ed., Lost World of the Aegean, Time-Life Books, New York, 1975

Finley, Moses I., The World of Odysseus. Viking, New York, 1954

Fitzgerald, Robert, trans., Homer's Iliad, Doubleday, New York and London, 1974

Furumark, Arne, Mycenaean Pottery, Stockholm, 1941

Greek Ministry of Culture, Troy: Heinrich Schliemann's Excavations and Finds, Athens, 1985

Wood, M., In Search of the Trojan War, Dutton, New York, 1989

H. DU THEIL

GODARE

# List of Illustrations

LIST OF ILLUSTRATIONS 139

# Index

# Acknowledgments

The publishers wish to thank the following for their help in preparing this book: Patrice Androussov, M. Bogdanov, Elias Eliadis, Alexandre Farnoux, Pierre de Gigord, Georges S. Korrès, and André Sidéris.

Hervé Duchêne,
a former member of the French School at Athens,
is Professor of Ancient History at the University
of Burgundy in Dijon. A specialist in Eastern
Mediterranean port and commercial archaeology,
he has been involved in excavations at Delos and
Thasos in Greece, working in the footsteps of the
archaeologists of the past one hundred years.
In *Notre Ecole Normale* (Belles-Lettres, 1994) he
brought fellow-archaeologist Salomon Reinach's
journals to the world's attention.

© Gallimard 1995

English translation © Thames and Hudson Ltd,
London, and Harry N. Abrams, Inc., New York, 1996

Translated by Jeremy Leggatt

British Library Cataloguing-in-Publication Data

A catalogue record for this book is available
from the British Library

ISBN 0-500-30065-8

Printed and bound in Italy
by Editoriale Libraria, Trieste